BABY IT'S YOU

BABY IT'S YOU

ANNETTE KARMILOFF-SMITH

EBURY PRESS

To Lesley
my cousin and very special friend

First published 1994

1 3 5 7 9 10 8 6 4 2

This paperback edition published in 1995 by Ebury Press
an imprint of Random House UK Ltd
Random House · 20 Vauxhall Bridge Road · London SW1V 2SA

Random House Australia (Pty) Limited
20 Alfred Street · Milsons Point · Sydney · New South Wales 2061 · Australia

Random House New Zealand Limited
18 Poland Road · Glenfield · Auckland 10 · New Zealand

Random House South Africa (Pty) Limited
PO Box 337 · Bergvlei · South Africa

Random House UK Limited Reg. No. 954009

BABY IT'S YOU
A Wall to Wall production for Channel 4
Executive producer Alex Graham
Produced by David Hickman
Directed by Leanne Klein

Designed by Martin Lovelock

A catalogue record for this book is available from the British Library.

ISBN: 0 09 180986 X

Printed by New Interlitho Italia S.p.A., Milan

The papers used by Ebury Press are natural, recyclable products made from wood grown in sustainable forests.

CONTENTS

PREFACE

When Alex Graham, Lin Brown and the team at Wall-to-Wall Television asked me if I would act as academic consultant to their new television series, *Baby It's You*, my first reaction was to shudder and reply: 'Oh no, not another programme about how cute babies are!' But they persuaded me at least to discuss the possibility over a glass of wine. Had they not agreed to meet me locally – in the café under London's oldest repertory cinema, the Everyman – I might have refused and missed out on a truly creative venture.

Leanne Klein and David Hickman (Director and Producer, respectively) quickly made me realize that the aim of the series was to present a very original approach to child development. For some years, the Executive Producer, Alex Graham, had cherished the idea of making a programme that would capture the world from the baby's point of view. Viewers weren't to be static observers of cute babies, but were to be drawn into the screen as if they themselves were the baby – hearing sounds, seeing images, progressively becoming a walker, a tool user, a talker, a thinker, and a social being. The series would contain no interviews with scientists nor demonstrations of child development research. Instead, the babies themselves would tell the story via the fascinating images of their spontaneous behaviours.

Leanne, David and I then embarked on a series of exciting brainstorming sessions, as we devised, revised and re-revised the scripts for the six programmes. We spent many creative evenings at my house, trying to penetrate the infant mind, to perceive and understand the world from her point of view. Leanne and David taught me a great deal about producing accessible yet captivating text and images that could be easily assimilated by viewers. I taught them about some of the paradoxes of development, e.g. that babies are often smarter than adults, and that there are real advantages to the

Far left: it is the Babinsky, or hand-to-mouth, reflex that drives the young baby to put his hand in his mouth.

helplessness of the human newborn, compared with other species which are up and running from birth. The fact that a baby's brain is not fully developed at birth allows far more plasticity – in other words, leaves it open to subsequent learning. We discussed new ideas about brain-behaviour relations and the nature/nurture debate, i.e. the issue of whether human language and intelligence are pre-programmed by nature, learned in the environment in which the infant grows up – or a complex interplay of both.

While the drafting of the scripts was progressing, two researchers, Helen Fletcher and Helena Ely, were sifting through the huge public response to advertisements for babies to appear in the television series. The letters and photographs were sorted into various categories, according to the baby's age, proximity for filming purposes, available space in the home for film crews and so forth. A tea party was held for the selected children and their parents, during which Alex explained the aims of the series and also why, as always, not all the filmed material would ultimately be used. Parents remained enthusiastic about participating, even though their particular baby might not end up on the TV screen. And they all expressed their willingness to fill in developmental diaries to record special changes and events in their baby's crawling, walking, language, intellectual and social behaviour.

The diaries formed an important part of the overall plans for the television series. Parents were asked to fill in a weekly set of sheets about various aspects of their baby's behaviour. First the diaries raised questions about the baby's sleeping and feeding patterns as well as about the moments when the baby was most alert. Second was a section about the baby's growing mobility: head lifting, rolling, sitting, crawling, standing, cruising holding onto furniture, and finally walking. The third sheet raised questions about the baby's dexterity in using her hands to manipulate tools. The fourth section of the diaries looked at communicative behaviours, from very early cooing, through the one-word stage, and on to the quite sophisticated sentences of the two- to three-year-olds. In the fifth section, questions were asked about the developing child's thinking abilities, starting from simple discoveries like the fact that shaking a rattle makes a noise, to the complex experiments that children carry out in their baths as they learn about water resistance and gravity. In the sixth section, parents were asked about children's developing social skills, how their baby interacts with other babies and adults, how aware she is of herself as an individual – say, of her reflection in

Far right: at only a few minutes old, the baby takes his first look at the world.

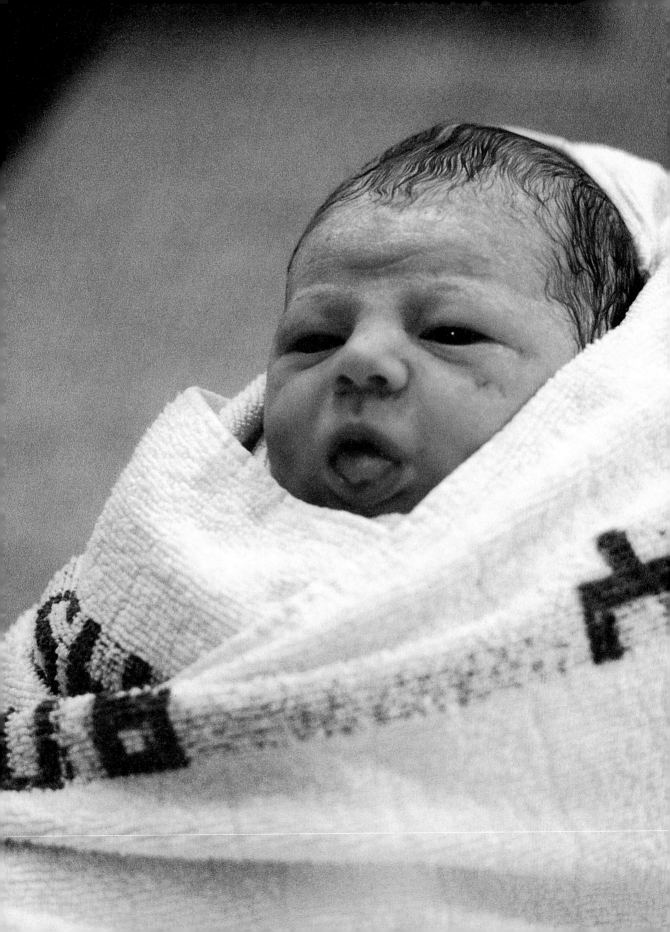

the mirror – and how aware she is of others as social partners. Finally there was a rag-bag section called 'Other' where parents could write down anything that didn't fit under the special headings but which they thought was particularly interesting. An example of the questionnaire can be found in an appendix at the back of the book.

Some parental reports were very short and to the point (e.g. 'Said two words today'). Others wrote little novels about their baby's progress, recording every possible detail. Both of these types of report were very useful for the television series because it allowed the film crew to visit babies at just the right moment of development. However, for the book, it is obviously the more expansive entries that made good illustrations for the reader. Wherever possible, I have quoted at least one entry from each parental diary, and in most cases several entries, and these are to be found throughout the book. In other cases I consulted my own diaries from years ago, as well as examples that have appeared in the developmental psychology literature. But the latter only represent 25 per cent of the examples in the book; the majority of the diary entries are directly from the parents who participated in setting up the television series, including those of babies who for various reasons did not actually appear in the programmes.

From the drafting of the scripts, Leanne and David moved on to filming. My role then switched to responding to frantic telephone calls asking how to get a recalcitrant two-month-old to demonstrate a behaviour that research described as the 'typical behaviour of two-month-olds'. Their two-month-old simply refused to perform! Of course, there's a wide gap between the spontaneous behaviour of a child at home and a child's behaviour in a structured experimental task with all other distractions removed.

It may be difficult for readers to imagine how one could possibly conduct experiments on pre-linguistic babies. How, for instance, can you tell whether babies recognise their mother tongue if they cannot yet utter a sound? How do you demonstrate that young infants are sensitive to numerical changes? How can you discover if babies can tell the difference between circles and squares? How is it possible to pinpoint young infants' sensitivity to certain physical laws, such as gravity? It is to the credit of a number of very talented developmental researchers that we now have answers to many such questions. At the end of the book is a brief section describing different types of experiments carried out with newborns and young babies.

Of course, experiments are carried out under very controlled

Far left: young babies are fascinated by objects, even those whose purpose they cannot begin to understand.

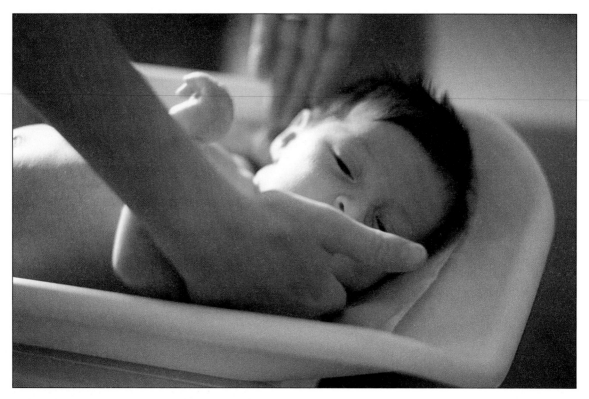

The newborn baby turns towards the hand that brushes her cheek – a demonstration of the rooting reflex essential for feeding.

conditions, with no other distractions. But in the naturalistic setting of a busy family home, it's really difficult to obtain the same behaviours. Yet David, Leanne and their film crew are to be congratulated on getting some astonishing shots of young infants' developmental patterns. Again and again, they skilfully managed to reduce the gap between experimental research and naturalistic behaviour.

As the filming of the series progressed, I watched Leanne and David peal away large amounts of the wording of the scripts. I was rapidly learning about the tight time constraints on television programmes. It then became clear that a book was an essential complement to the series. Now, academics take anything between two to five years to write a book. The media world expected me to write an entire book in three months! But I was anyway busy with my academic research. The solution that Ebury Press came up with was to employ someone to whom we could give the scripts and research notes, and to whom I could dictate all the relevant extra material, so that an unstructured first draft could be quickly produced for me to work from. The new member of the team was a charming young mother, Lola Borg, who knew just what I meant when we got to the section about how all family life centres around the newborn's needs! We were all set to go.

Then, what seemed like a calamity occurred. I suddenly had to spend a long period in hospital, followed by convalescence at home. Actually, this turned out – for both the television series and the book – to be a blessing in disguise. For the first time in my professional life I was constantly reachable on the phone, and there was little else I could manage to do than talk. So I dictated on the phone the notes for a whole book! There are many delightful photographs that accompany the text of this book, taken by Steve Lovell-Davis during the filming of the series. But an amusing photograph not included is the one of me, flat on my back in my hospital bed, with tubes coming out from all sides, telephone balanced on the pillow as I spent hours telling Lola about child-development research and brain/behaviour relations. She recorded the telephone tutorials and got the rough material on paper in record time. We were only interrupted by the occasional nurse coming to take my temperature and blood pressure. This was clearly a first for the doctors and nurses – and for me!

When academics realise they can't meet a deadline, it is simply

The ability to lift her head gives the young baby a new view of the world

postponed to a later date. We set our own schedules. Not so in the world of books accompanying TV series. They have to be out on a specific date and no other. As time got tighter and my health allowed me to get back to my own research, it became clear that evening and weekend book-writing was insufficient to meet the tight deadline. With only two weeks to go, we brought in another team member: one of my talented young colleagues at the MRC Cognitive Development unit, Geoff Hall, a psychology PhD from Harvard University. Geoff read the television scripts and the material I had dictated to Lola, agreed to check through the chapters already completed and undertake the last-minute redrafting of sections of the remaining ones so that I could then rework them into the style of the rest of the book. His contribution was absolutely invaluable as the deadline loomed. Meanwhile, Lola had extracted the delightful quotations from the parents' developmental diaries so that they could be inserted throughout the text. Ríona MacNamara from Ebury Press and my daughter, Kyra Karmiloff, helped me make the selection from Steve Lovell-Davis's enchanting photographs and write the captions. Ríona was on the phone to me daily chasing the writing I'd produced the evening before. I often wondered when she thought I might sleep! Martin Lovelock did a splendid design on the book.

The book is the result of all our endeavours – Leanne's, David's, Alex's, Lin's, Geoff's, Lola's, Kyra's, Ríona's, Stephen's, Martin's and mine.

Obviously this book isn't intended to be an academic textbook on child development. It is for the general reader, for anyone fascinated by how babies perceive their world. For this reason, it did not seem appropriate to end the book with a long list of references to articles in learned journals. Yet obviously the material in both the television series and the book benefited from the work of many talented developmentalists in the field. The researchers whose work was used either directly or indirectly are acknowledged in the list of names at the end of the book, with sincere apologies for any unwitting omissions. Special mention should also be made of the British Psychological Society Developmental Section's worldwide electronic mail network, centred at the University of Durham. I sent out on the network a list of questions raised by Leanne and David for the television series that were outside my particular area of expertise, and I was overwhelmed by the rapid responses from developmentalists all over the world.

Far left: the newborn baby has abilities that allow her to be happy and confident underwater.

I stressed above that the book is not intended to be an academic textbook. But nor is it your typical parental guide to babies, either. On the contrary. The book stems from the original aims of the television series, *Baby It's You*, to understand the world from the baby's viewpoint. A typical example of this is to be found in Chapter 2. For parents, the moment when their babies stand and take their first step is a major landmark. For babies, by contrast, the moment when they first manage to get a different view of the world by lifting their head is probably just as important. And the comments in the developmental diaries bear witness to infants' real sense of achievement each time they discover a new behaviour. The diaries were not originally intended for publication, but rather as a research support to the television series. However, they turned out to be so delightful that we persuaded parents – including those whose babies did not appear in the series – to have their unedited extracts reproduced in the book.

I was faced with the dilemma of whether to call the infant 'it', 'he' or 'she'. The use of 'she or he'/'him or her'/'hers or his' made the text unnecessarily heavy. The solution I chose was as follows. The foetus is referred to as 'it'. Wherever it was possible stylistically, I used the plural to refer to babies, but as a female professional with two delightful daughters I of course decided on 'she' when I needed to refer to the baby in the singular. But before male readers object, note that I do frequently mention fathers and not just the maternal role in child rearing. Throughout the book approximate ages are given with respect to when babies reach various developmental milestones. These should be considered as a rough guide only; some perfectly normally developing babies will acquire skills much earlier or later than others.

I have done my best to keep the developmental concepts simple, yet not simplistic. Above all, I have tried to draw the reader into the extraordinarily exciting journey that we all once made as we slowly progressed from the moment of conception into our final form as adults with fully developed brains.

The human brain results from millions of years of evolution. But it would be wrong to think that infants are totally pre-programmed. Nor are they totally un-programmed. Our genes provide pre-dispositions for specific kinds of learning, but during development babies actually structure their brains via their experiences in the world. In other words, babies are born with the hundred thousand million brain cells that will be used (or not used) for everything they

Far right: when their first 'smiles' get positive results from people around them, babies soon learn to give genuine smiles of pleasure.

do in subsequent life. But they are not born with the million billion connections that link cells and form complex brain circuits. These connections are the result of development. And as different parts of the brain progressively mature and allow for new behaviours, so the practice of those behaviours structures the brain in return. Nature and development are far more dynamic and interactive than previous theories gave credit. If there's a God, she left a lot of work to us!

There is a dramatic fact about babies which is often referred to in the following chapters: what seem to an adult observer to be random movement or mere play actually constitute serious work on the part of the infant. Take a look at a young baby and you will see that she is constantly moving her arms and legs, whether in her cot or in a bath. Video that activity, and speed it up by fast-forwarding the tape, and you'll be struck by the strenuous workout in which the infant is relentlessly engaged. Watch somewhat older babies, and you'll quickly discover that they spend much of their playtime exploring physical laws and social conventions. We tend to think of babyhood as a period of helplessness and idle play. In fact, being a baby is very hard work, because she is fired by a relentless drive to become a fully fledged, walking, tool-using, talking, thinking, social being. This is what the following chapters are all about.

My life as a developmental cognitive scientist is just like a baby's – there's no real division between work and play. That's why my collaboration with the *Baby It's You* television and book projects has been such fun.

Annette Karmiloff-Smith
London, January 1994.

Far left: the ability to sit unaided gives the baby a new view on the world.

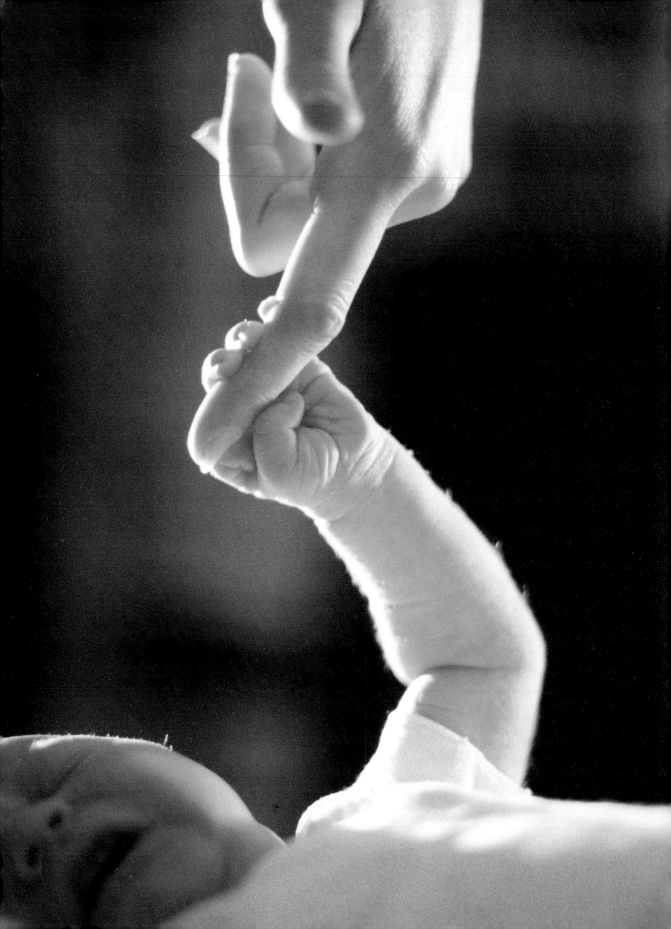

CHAPTER ONE

BORN TO LEARN

This book is about a journey – the journey of a traveller who starts out as a mere mass of muscle, tissue, water, and nerves, and ends up as a fully-fledged human being. All the mundane skills that we use as adults, the skills that you are taking for granted at this very moment as you read – sitting on a chair, holding the book, turning the pages, reading the words, looking at the photographs, making sense of what you're seeing – once had to be learnt from scratch.

But there's a paradox about development. Sometimes babies are smarter than adults! We'll see illustrations of this throughout the

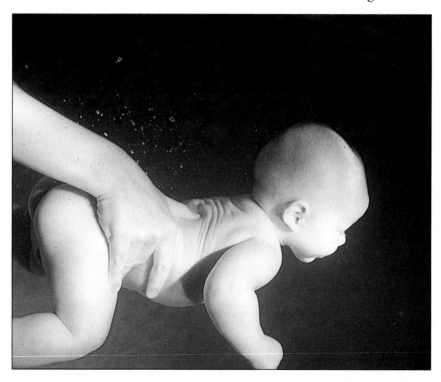

Even when only a few hours old, this newborn baby won't risk drowning; she can close off the tract leading to her lungs and keep her mouth and eyes wide open as she swims – an ability she'll lose later in life. **Far left:** the newborn demonstrates the grasping reflex.

book. For example, although helpless in their cots, newborns are far from helpless underwater. They have an ability to swim by making frog-like movements to propel themselves forward. Underwater their eyes and mouths gape open, but they have no chance of drowning because their throats and the tract leading to the lungs shut off automatically on contact with the water. This is something they won't be able to do later.

But although behaviours like underwater swimming are pre-programmed from our evolutionary past, most of human development is not. In particular, one part of the tiny newborn baby will undergo enormous changes: the brain. Even though the brain already has the 100 billion cells it will need throughout life, a million billions of essential connections between cells will develop only progressively as a function of the baby's experience. This is a fundamental idea: development is a constant interaction between the emerging structure of the brain and the baby's experiences in the world. Babies are not passive. They actively participate in the structuring of their own development. They are born to learn.

At birth the baby is faced with the most exciting of challenges: to transform herself from a helpless, reflex-bound organism into a walking, talking, thinking, social being. Learning begins from the moment of birth – and even before.

IN THE WOMB

In the last three months of intra-uterine life, the foetus is already learning. Not only can it turn, move its legs, arms, and hands, and grip the umbilical cord, it also practises some of the basic reflexes which will later affect its behaviour. Foetuses suck their thumbs in the womb: they are already working on an important reflex – the sucking reflex – which they will need for feeding. Although sight isn't useful in the gloom of the uterus, the foetus already opens and closes its eyes, the action being a precursor to its later blinking reflex. Well before birth it is gradually becoming aware of the different parts of its own body.

At the same time, the foetus is responding to the world outside its mother. From about three months before birth, if a bright torch is shone on to the womb the foetus reacts by moving suddenly. It is also aware of changes in pressure, even while floating in amniotic liquid. If a heavy book is placed on its mother's stomach, the foetus responds to the pressure and pushes against it with its shoulders, elbows or knees. An entry from one of the mothers who filled out the developmental diaries provides a nice example:

> **Dianne's mother (seven months pregnant):** I was desperately trying to get some work finished before the birth and was in bed reading a manual about my new computer. At one point I rested the book on my stomach. I couldn't believe it. Next thing I knew I could see the outline of the baby's elbow (well, I think it was its elbow) sticking right out of my stomach, trying to push the book away. My husband made some sexist remark about the baby not wanting Mummy to work, and I dug him in the ribs!

Although sight isn't useful in the womb, sound is. The foetus can hear, although what it hears is filtered and muffled. Sounds from the world outside have to compete with the echoing beat of its mother's heart, the rumbling of the amniotic fluid, as well as with the amplified sounds of its mother's other internal organs. The foetus also hears its mother's voice and already starts to become familiar with the tone, pitch and intonation patterns, even though the sound is different from what it will hear after it is born. For the time being, its mother's heartbeat is louder than her voice.

Research in the last ten years has shown just how much the foetus can learn in the womb. For example, if its mother repeatedly reads aloud the same story during the last three months of pregnancy, then when it is born the baby will prefer hearing that story to an unfamiliar one. Of course, this doesn't mean that it understands the story. But the infant's preference for that story demonstrates the sensitivity to the pattern of words and intonation that the foetus built up in the womb. The developmental diaries give a colourful example of the foetus' attention to conversation:

> **Dianne's mother (eight months pregnant):** I was having a heated discussion about women's role in society with this thick man who still thinks of women as household objects. I was getting increasingly loud, and I could feel the baby moving more and more. It seemed even to move to his voice, when he shouted back – I suppose it can hear other people through my ears? Then afterwards when I sat down to rest, the baby seemed to stop moving. Amazing!

Experiments have also been done with music. If certain tunes are played to the foetus (in the experiments, these were the themes from various soap operas such as *Neighbours* and *Eastenders*), then at birth the baby will show a preference for listening to the familiar music rather than an unfamiliar tune.

Foetuses have even been shown to discriminate between various classical composers. If its mother repeatedly listens to different pieces by Mozart, the foetus will initially react by kicking vigorously in the womb. However, as the foetus gets used to hearing Mozart again and again, its kicking lessens as it becomes increasingly familiar with that music, and then stops. If the mother then switches to Bach, however, the foetus will start vigorously kicking again. This is not just a discrimination between two different pieces of music, one by Bach, one by Mozart. What happens is that with time the foetus recognises the different Mozart pieces as all having something in common. The Bach piece provokes renewed kicking, not because it is different from one particular piece by Mozart, but because it is different from something similar in *all* the pieces by Mozart. Here again, babies may be smarter than adults. It's not certain that all adults would show such sensitivity to the differences among classical composers. The diaries provide a nice example of the foetus reacting to music:

> **Dianne's mother (seven-and-a-half months pregnant):** Every night Jack and I have a quiet moment after work playing our favourite Mahler. For us it's the quiet moment, but not for the baby! It moves around constantly – maybe it's because the volume is loud, but it doesn't seem to move like that when we watch the news on TV.

These various experiments indicate that the foetus can already discriminate among many different types of stimuli. However, the precise characteristics of what it recognises are not known, and they are probably relatively simple. What is known is that foetuses are able to discern a feature common to the different stimuli and react to a change in that feature. Moreover, they like to listen to what they've already heard; they prefer it to the unfamiliar. Such research indicates that learning doesn't just begin the moment the baby comes into the world; it starts in the womb.

Although the foetus is actively learning, it is still part of its mother's body. Indeed, the foetus is very aware of its mother's body. It knows something of her mood changes and is affected by them. It can sense if she is anxious or relaxed. But this communication between mother and foetus is not one-sided. She too is sensitive to the foetus's changing states. Moreover, the foetus is even responsible for triggering its own birth. At the point it is capable of survival in the outside world, it releases into its mother's bloodstream a hormone that sets off labour.

BIRTH

For nine months the foetus has shared its mother's physiology. Now, as the baby breathes for the first time using her own lungs, she is a separate biological organism. The cutting of the umbilical cord is the beginning of her journey to becoming an independent human being.

Birth is a traumatic experience for the baby. During her first hour in the world, the baby is more alert and wide-eyed than she will be for days to come. There are two reasons for this. One is related to the shock of the extraordinary experience she has just had. From the

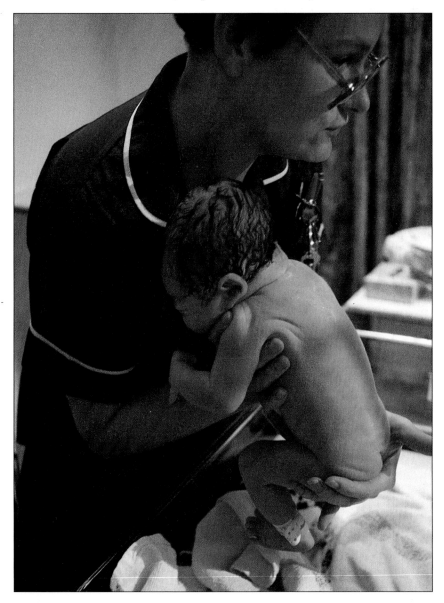

The newborn's floppy body needs to be completely supported at all times. Here the baby is about to be tested for heart and respiratory rates, muscle tone and response to stimulation.

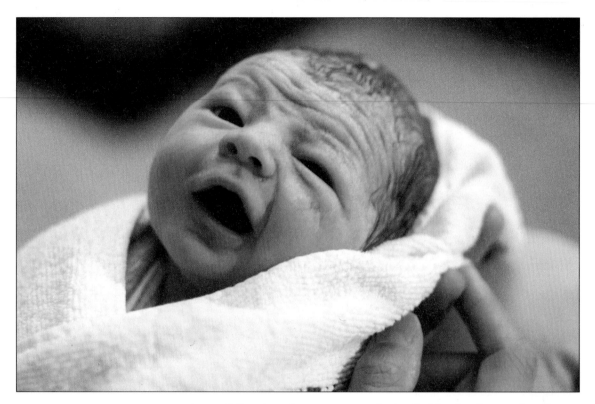

A few minutes old and the newborn is in a kind of hyperstate with all her senses alert to cope with the bombardment of new experiences. This is the perfect time for researchers to experiment on young babies.

comfort of floating in warm amniotic fluid, the foetus has been forced down a narrow birth canal into a cold, bright and unfamiliar world. The second reason why the newborn is so alert is that, during birth, her adrenaline level soars to twice that of her mother's – whose level is already very high. The baby's level of adrenaline is even higher than that of someone suffering a heart attack. Yet the elevated amount of adrenaline is not damaging. On the contrary. It is useful, not just for coping with the considerable trauma of birth but also for setting the baby's newly separated body into independent motion, for getting the heart, liver, lungs and all the bodily organs working on their own.

The newborn is in a kind of hyper-state with all her senses alert to cope with the bombardment of new experiences. For this reason, certain tests on newborns are done within the first hour or two after delivery. The most common of these tests provides the Apgar score which indicates the efficiency of the heart and respiratory rates, muscle tone, response to stimulation and colour. This is administered at one and five minutes after the birth. And many exciting new discoveries about newborn capacities are based on research also done within the first few hours. For infancy researchers

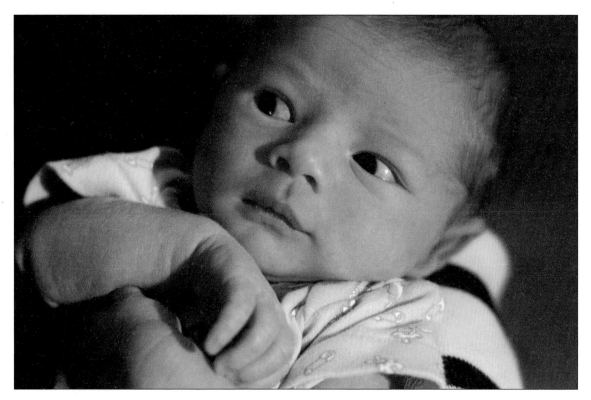

devising experiments on the newborn, a five-hour-old baby is a very old baby indeed! The baby's adrenaline levels revert to normal after a couple of hours, allowing her to recover and sleep off her ordeal.

SLEEPING

The newborn spends most of her time sleeping. She can remain asleep for between sixteen and eighteen hours – even as many as 23 hours a day. Feeding takes up most of the remainder of the day, along with brief but growing spells of alert wakefulness. The following two entries attest to these alternations between sleep and alertness:

> **Xavier (two weeks):** Sleeps approximately 3-4 hours daytime between feeds with periods of alertness following objects with his eyes from side to side around the room.

> **Holly (seven weeks):** Each week Holly spends more and more time awake and alert. Luckily she seems to have fitted into a pattern of sleeping at night, waking sometimes once or at the most twice.

Newborns spend the first four to six weeks of their lives perfecting this cycle of behaviour, separating sleep states from waking states,

A few hours after birth and the baby is already actively scanning the environment – seeing new things, listening to new sounds, smelling new odours – and learning to cope with an enormous influx of new information.

31

Long periods of sleep
are essential for the
baby to switch off from
external stimulation and
for the brain to
reorganise its recent
experiences.

establishing routines and settling into the world of noises, light, smell and touch outside the womb.

It may seem curious to argue that sleeping is a way for the baby to be in control. After all, she doesn't seem to be doing anything at all! In fact, sleep is the perfect opportunity for the baby to switch off from external stimulation and for her brain to reorganise its recent experiences. Babies sleep twice as much as adults, though babies' sleep periods are broken into much shorter spells than adults'. Like adults', babies' sleep is organised into different phases. There is quiet sleep – a deep and almost totally motionless sleep. There is also REM (Rapid Eye Movement) sleep, characterised by the eyes flickering under closed lids and an increase in heart rate and blood pressure. It is associated with dreaming in adults. Babies have twice as much REM sleep as adults, and they seem to be dreaming too. Indeed, they often waken startled, as if they've had a bad dream. It is impossible to know for sure whether babies actually do dream, and if they do what on earth they might dream about! But whatever the function of babies' REM sleep, the sleep cycle is very important for normal development:

> **Martin (four weeks):** I've noticed when Martin is sleeping that his face goes suddenly all red and his eyelids seem to be moving all the time – like he's having a bad dream or something. Then he seems to go all quiet for a while, and then he starts moving again.

In this period of rapid learning and new experiences, the baby's brain needs time to reorganise and form new connections among brain cells as a result of the wealth of new information she is receiving. Periods of sleep can allow the baby to sort out some of that chaotic input. Babies often go to sleep in order to shut out external stimulation. It gives them time to integrate new experiences. Occasionally, babies even 'flat line' during sleep – that is, their brain activity effectively ceases, crashing like a computer in overload, only to reboot itself automatically microseconds later.

MOVEMENT AND REFLEXES

Unlike other mammals, indeed unlike any other animal, the human baby is woefully helpless at birth. Horses, dogs and lions can get up and walk within hours of being born, but human babies are incapable of virtually any intentional movement. Their bones are soft and rubbery, their muscles weak and watery. They can't move their heavy, oversized heads and their arms and legs jerk in an uncontrolled way. Here's a comment from the developmental diaries showing how much very tiny babies constantly move around:

> **Xavier (seven weeks):** Jerky movements, kicks one leg when feeding. Makes fists and sometimes clasps them together on his chest. Puts fist in mouth.

But babies are born with a set of reflexes to help them through the first weeks of life; indeed, some are vital for survival. Babies have reflexes similar to the knee-jerk and the blinking reflexes in adults. When hit on the knee, an adult's leg jolts forward, and his eye shuts rapidly if something is about to be poked into it. These reactions are totally involuntary. Indeed, it is virtually impossible to avoid making

Compared to other species, the human newborn is helpless and a few minutes after birth is still curled up in the foetal position, with jerky, uncontrolled movements.

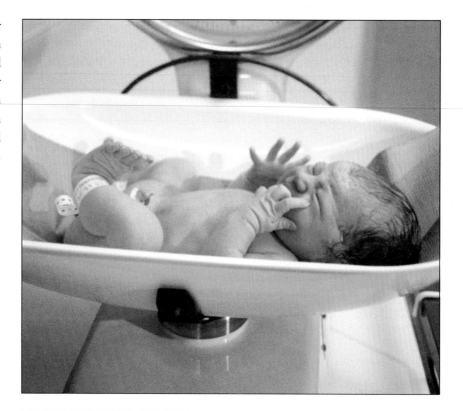

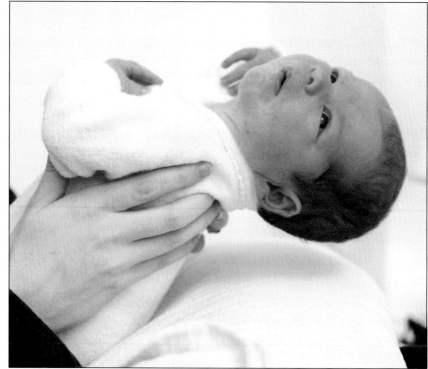

But unlike other species his brain is disproportionately large and heavy, and it will take several months before he can control his head and neck movements.

the automatic response of a reflex. Breathing is obviously one of the most important reflexes for a baby. But babies also need the rooting and sucking reflexes to help them get nourishment. Without these reflexes, the baby would have difficulty surviving. The rooting and sucking reflexes can be provoked if a baby's cheek is gently stroked. She will automatically turn in the direction of the touch and pucker her mouth to suck. So if the mother's breast brushes against the baby's face, she will immediately turn to feed. And the baby is not always fussy about what she starts to feed on:

> **Martin (three weeks):** Martin is so anxious to feed at times that he sucks at anything he gets his mouth around – even the buttons on my dress.

Although these are called reflexes – and they are – it would be a mistake to assume that they remain rigid action patterns. In fact, the behaviour initially provoked by the reflexes improves with development. Despite the fact that babies automatically turn to suck if their cheeks are stroked, they gradually learn to suck a particular nipple – their mother's or the one on their bottle. The baby is born with the reflex, but women are not all born with the same shape, size or height of nipple. Rubber teats come in all shapes and sizes, too. Yet the baby learns to suck very efficiently, whether nipples are big, small, elongated or practically inverted. Each time she sucks, the baby does so better than the time before. It is the same with the tracking reflex which causes babies to follow any moving object. Initially, they overshoot or undershoot the object by jerking their eyes too quickly or too slowly to follow it properly. But with practice – and they practise relentlessly – their tracking skills improve. So what started as a simple reflex soon takes on a more complex form, as the diaries show:

> **Sarah (three and a half months):** Sarah used to fiddle about trying to get my nipple into her mouth and would let go of it by mistake while feeding and start crying. But nowadays she goes straight for it without any hesitation, as if she knows in advance where to aim for, and if I'm not careful she takes a sharp bite into it!

There are other reflexes, too, several of which will be discussed in more detail in the chapters to follow. The Babinksy, or hand-to-mouth, reflex drives the baby to place her clenched fist in her mouth from birth. With another reflex – the walking reflex – the new baby will appear to be walking if her feet are placed just in contact with a

The rooting reflex: when the baby's cheek is stroked he will immediately turn his head and pucker his lips to feed. Like all newborn reflexes, this has roots in our evolutionary past.

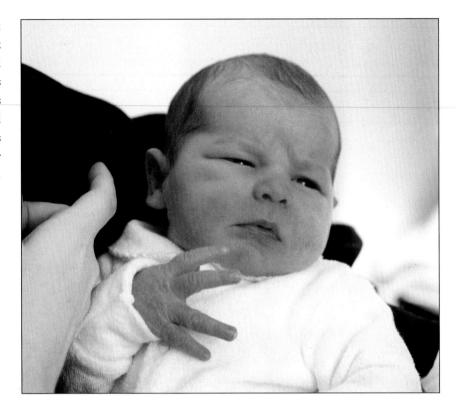

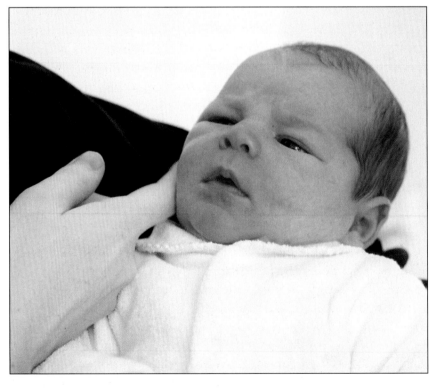

hard surface. The grasping reflex can be seen if the baby is touched lightly on the palm of her hand. She will immediately curl her fingers and grip hard. The reflex is so strong that if an adult puts a finger in each of the baby's palms, the baby can be lifted by her arms and will support her own weight. Here's an amusing comment from the parental diaries:

> **Laura (3 weeks):** Laura has an incredibly strong grip. Sometimes I can't get my finger away from her. One of the researchers on the programme told me I could hang her from the washing line and her grip would hold her up, but I lost my nerve!

Ironically, the hardest thing for babies to learn is to let go – their fingers have to be prised open. Letting go requires voluntary control which must await certain developments in the brain. The stepping and grasping reflexes seem to disappear in the weeks after birth, but similar behaviours of a more voluntary type reappear later, also as a result of subsequent brain development.

The Babinsky reflex drives the baby to place her clenched fist in her mouth. This is the precursor to mouthing, through which the baby will later begin to discover the shapes and textures of objects.

HEARING

The baby comes into the world already familiar with many different

 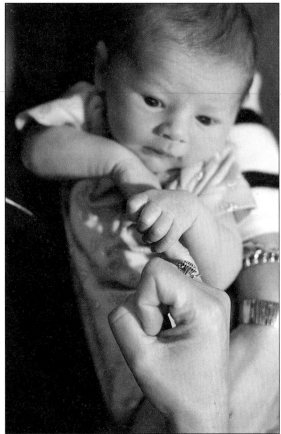

Newborns are sometimes smarter than older babies. At birth the baby demonstrates the walking reflex **(above)**, something which he will later lose. The grasping reflex **(above right)** is strong and once newborn babies grasp something they cannot voluntarily let go.

types of sound. During the final three months in the womb, the foetus hears the beat of all its mother's organs as well as the intonation of her voice and the rhythmic sounds of the amniotic liquid.

At birth, the baby's hearing system is almost as sensitive as an adult's. The anatomy for hearing is already mature (in fact, the only fully-grown bones in the baby's body are those in the middle ear). However, babies' hearing thresholds are somewhat lower than adults', which is why newborns can happily sleep through a consistently blaring television or very loud music. But sudden changes in noise levels do disturb them: a door banging or a telephone ringing, for example, will sometimes make them cry. The diaries provide a couple of examples:

Dianne (one week): I've been studying the way Dianne sleeps to keep note of everything she does. One thing I've noticed is that some noises really disturb her and others – like the dishwasher which bothers me if I'm trying to read – doesn't seem to bother her at all – she doesn't even seem to notice and sleeps on peacefully.

Julia (three weeks): Funny what wakes her up. Sometimes we have the TV on quite loud and she doesn't even stir. Then the front door bell will ring and she'll wake up startled and start to cry.

Babies prefer to hear soothing rhythmic noises that echo the sounds they heard in the womb: the swish of a washing machine, the drone of a vacuum cleaner or a hairdryer, 'white noise' such as an untuned radio or television. All these are particularly calming, presumably because they seem familiar – and therefore comforting – in an unfamiliar world. As we've seen, babies favour what they've been used to in the womb and prefer familiar music and words over unfamiliar ones.

What elicits the greatest response, though, is the sound of a human voice. It takes the newborn only three to four days to recognise her mother's voice and distinguish its pitch and tone from those of other people. A baby will quieten and turn towards the sound of a human voice, particularly one speaking her mother tongue – a very useful strategy that helps her link voices to faces and build a more rounded picture of the people around her. The parental diaries show how babies become particularly attentive to human voices:

Dianne (three weeks): Whenever Jack and I are chatting, the baby seems to react. She stiffens her body a bit and looks in our direction – as if something important was happening. I've been reading about this sort of thing and it's true – she really reacts to our voices.

Laura (five weeks): I've the impression that Laura turns her head especially when she hears Dereck's or my voice. The TV doesn't seem to get the same reaction from her.

Babies especially like being spoken to in the exaggerated, high-pitched, sing-song voice that adults automatically adopt when talking to young children. The vowel sounds are stretched out ('Hellooo Little Baaay...Beee, you're sooooo loverrrly!'), and every sentence sounds as though it ends with an exclamation mark. Babies lose interest when an adult switches from such high-pitched intonation to making a comment to another adult in a normal voice. Indeed, research has shown that babies prefer babytalk, or 'motherese', to normal speech. If babies are placed in front of two speakers, one producing motherese and the other adult-like conversation, they will consistently look towards the speaker emitting motherese. Here is a mother's comment about the naturalness of this type of language:

> **Evelyn (ten months):** I keep trying to speak to her normally – but it's odd, I find myself quite naturally talking in a sing-song voice whenever I'm with her. When one of my friends is there, I try to talk normally. You feel such an idiot. Yet somehow it just comes out, like there was a special language for babies that we never have to learn. I've noticed people in the street do it too. The newsagent does it the most – a real piece of opera whenever he sees Evelyn.

So young infants know a lot about language well before they themselves ever produce anything vaguely resembling speech. At birth, they can distinguish music from human language, although both are sounds. After only four days, they are even able to distinguish their own mother tongue from other languages. A four-day-old English baby may not be able to distinguish French from Spanish, but she will differentiate English from French and English from Spanish. Of course the baby won't understand the meaning. However, she has learnt something about the intonation and contours of the language she has been regularly listening to. This is impressively quick learning. All these factors suggest that the human baby arrives in the world especially attuned to other people.

TASTE AND SMELL

The senses of taste and smell are present at birth. Although the taste buds become more refined with age, babies a few days old already smile when given sweet things (which they prefer) and grimace at bitter or salty ones. Newborns are very sensitive to smell, too. They can remember certain smells from the very first day of life and show a strong preference for their parents' natural odour. And here's another example of babies being smarter than adults: just a few hours after birth, a baby can distinguish the smell of her own mother's milk from that of other mothers. Adults can't tell the difference and judge all maternal milks as roughly equivalent. The newborn's sense of smell is so acute that researchers testing young babies' abilities in face recognition experiments have to deodorise mothers to ensure that babies don't use smell alone to recognise them.

Some comments in the developmental diaries point to this early sensitivity to smell:

> **Dianne (three weeks):** I've noticed that when I wear Cabochard (my favourite perfume), the baby seems to smile ... or she might

be grimacing because it's not her favourite perfume! She seems to react to smells though.

Sarah (four months): Sarah seems to recognise the smell when we're having spinach.

VISION

Until the moment when babies first open their eyes and confront the stark environment of the delivery room or home, sight has not been of much use. However, babies' vision develops rapidly from birth when they are suddenly bombarded with stimuli. At first, however, they see quite poorly. An adult with similar sight would be registered as visually impaired and given a white stick! The baby's focus is limited to objects less than a metre away. The baby can see in colour (though she may not yet be able to see the colour blue), but her world looks slightly out of focus and lacks definition, rather as if everything were seen through a mist. Also, the images from the

Although the foetus opens and closes its eyes in the womb, practising the blinking reflex, its first real use of its eyes is in the delivery room at the moment of birth. But although we now know that the baby is capable of distinguishing objects and most colours, her focus is limited to people and objects less than a metre away.

retinas of the baby's eyes haven't yet merged, so the world appears as if seen through two separate tunnels.

In alert moments, newborns are constantly moving their eyes, seeking out visual stimulation. However, initially their eye movements are slow and jerky and at first they are attracted more to stimuli in the periphery than in front of them. Research has shown that newborn babies have distinct preferences for what they look at. The first is movement. All recent research indicates that a newborn baby is designed to be attracted to and actively seek out moving objects. This sensitivity to movement might have evolutionary roots, giving babies early warning of the presence of moving predators. But it also draws babies to look at things which best stimulate the developing visual areas of their brains. Sensitivity to movement is also useful because one of the most interesting objects babies will come across – other humans – isn't at all static. A second visual preference is for very high-contrast objects, such as those that are striped or chequered. Babies are also attracted by objects with curvilinear surfaces which move, of which the human face is a perfect example, as we can see from the diaries:

> **Julia (eight weeks):** Sometimes Julia won't stop looking at my face – she stares and stares, and even when I shake the rattle or the teddy bear, she still keeps looking at my face. It's uncanny.

> **Benji (ten weeks):** He seems to watch my face a lot. But not just mine. When Raj picks him up, he fixes on his face too. Even when I take him out in the pram to the park, he watches people's faces when they look into his pram. He seems to find faces the most interesting thing, more than other things.

Research has shown that babies are born with a very simple mental template of the human face and will actually search out and stare at human faces during their first two months of life. So from the outset, the baby is designed to be attracted to the very object that will take care of her and help her learn the most: the face of her mother or father. Babies focus best on things at eight to ten inches away. So when cradled in her mother's arms, the baby is at the perfect distance to see her in focus, whilst the rest of the potentially distracting world fades into a blur.

To determine precisely when babies really recognise their parents is no easy matter, and there is much controversy amongst infancy researchers in this field. Some believe that babies recognise their

Whatever their age, babies are fascinated by faces, and by two months start to recognise the internal features of familiar ones.

mothers during the first week of life; others argue that the infant cannot recognise individual faces – mother's or anyone else's – until about two months. Recent thinking divides face recognition into several different mechanisms.

First, there is a general pattern recognition device that the baby is born with. This will attract it to symmetrical or other regular and contrastive patterns. Such a mechanism is thought to be used by the infant to recognise the general shape of her mother's head. She

From the moment of birth the baby is drawn to human faces. The newborn will stare for hours at his mother's face, but really recognises her only by the overall shape of her face and hairline.

doesn't yet recognise the internal features of her mother's face. In other words, the baby may initially recognise her own mother simply by her hairline and the outline of her face. If her mother puts on a hat or cuts her hair, the baby may well be confused.

Second is a mechanism specialised in recognising the internal features of human faces in general, but not individual faces. This device will attract young infants to any objects that resemble a human face. Present them with three dark blobs on a white oval, in the same configuration as the human face, and the very young baby will be just as fascinated.

A third mechanism develops around two months of age and is used by babies to recognise individual people. Now they prefer real faces to three blobs. They can start analysing the internal features of faces, so by this point the baby really does know her mother's face. The mother could cut her hair, wear sunglasses or put on a hat and this wouldn't disconcert the baby. By this point, of course, the baby is also beginning to know much more generally about her mother – her voice, her shape, her gait, her behaviour. So as well as recognising a certain configuration of nose, eyes, mouth, face-shape and hair, the baby is building quite a complex mental image of her mother.

Faces are not the only thing of interest to babies. They also begin to pay attention to the objects in their world. They are born with what are called 'innate scan paths'. When they look at an object, they flick their eyes back and forth around the edges. With development of the visual system, however, the internal features of objects – toys, furniture and, of course, faces – become the baby's focus of attention. At the same time, visual tracking – following moving objects with the eyes – becomes more deliberate. Show the baby a ball, and she may look at it for a while and get bored. Throw the same ball in the air, though, and the baby will immediately track it. The diaries give some examples of this interest in moving objects:

> **Dianne (four weeks):** Dianne is fascinated by Miranda's train set (Miranda = older sister). She follows it round the track with her eyes and never seems to tire of watching it go around.

> **Martin (seven weeks):** We were having a picnic near a fairground and he seemed to be completely engrossed in watching the big-wheel from his pushchair.

After six to eight weeks, the baby seems to switch into a different gear and her visual examinations of the world begin to change. At four weeks, the baby's attention is focused on where things are; she tracks anything moving and notes its final location. At about eight weeks, the baby focuses on what things are. She now begins to study objects more carefully and to look at their finer details.

Also of interest is the fact that early on, once babies look intently at an interesting face or object, they have difficulty disengaging. In other words, the only way they can move their focus of attention is with the help of an adult distracting them. The diaries give one such example:

> **Benji (seven weeks):** It's sometimes really hard to get Benji's attention – he seems to get stuck watching his mobile and you can't get him to look away. Sometimes I have to shake his rattles quite hard right in front of his face to get his attention back.

By three or four months of age, babies can easily disengage attention on their own. The pathways in the brain for voluntary action are starting to take over. Then babies can inhibit obligatory looking and choose what they want to look at and to explore.

INTERPRETING THE WORLD OF OBJECTS

Our adult brains automatically make sense of what we see. As an example, glance around the room you are in now. Imagine how confusing it would seem without our basic perceptual tools. We know that a door is three-dimensional even though it might appear, to the eye, to be completely flat. We also recognise that a coffee cup is a separate object from the table it happens to be sitting on. If a vase of flowers is moved from the end of the room to a table directly in front of us, we don't mistake it for a different vase. It may look much larger on the retina, but we interpret it as the same one. Likewise, the same vase of flowers viewed from above, from one side, or from another appears to be a completely different object, yet we continue to interpret it as the same.

But what about the baby? For a long time it was thought that the newborn perceives and interprets objects in a kind of chaotic, surreal way, famously described by the early twentieth-century psychologist,

Human babies are not just interested in faces: the whole world of objects will be a constant source of stimulation and exploration for them.

William James, as the infant's 'buzzing, blooming confusion'. But recent research suggests that the infant's world, although blurred, isn't that different from the adults'.

It is known that babies can see the objects around them, but how do they interpret what they see? Recent research has shown that many of the visual interpretations we make as adults are already part of the human brain potential at birth and enable babies to start to make sense of their world. They don't, of course, know that a table is a table or a vase is a vase. That's part of learning. But the baby does seem to perceive tables, vases and the like as three-dimensional objects, with edges, surfaces, specific shapes and textures.

According to many researchers, babies know a lot about size, shape and depth from the very beginning. After about five days, babies will only reach for things like mobiles that are within their grasp. Also, when an object moves towards the baby, it appears to get bigger and to change shape, but she will treat it as the same object. Imagine the baby's father shaking a teddy-bear in the air and bringing it down towards her face. As the teddy-bear comes closer and closer, the image it makes on her retina becomes larger, and could be potentially frightening. But the baby's apparent lack of fear suggests that she perceives the depth cues and considers the teddy-bear to be the same one throughout. Experiments with young infants have pointed to the same conclusion.

Not only do babies understand size constancy, they understand shape constancy too. They will know that if an object is rotated or moved, it will only appear to be different, it won't actually be different. An important consequence of this is that the baby doesn't think her mother is a different person each time she turns her head and she sees her in profile.

THE BRAIN

Over the first twelve months of life, the baby's brain will grow more rapidly than any other part of her body, tripling its volume and reaching three quarters of its adult size by the time she is one. Every brain cell – or neuron – that the baby will ever use throughout life is present at birth. But unlike most other species, few cells in the human baby's brain are already fixed in their specialist functions. In fact, at birth, the human brain is less organised than the brain of virtually any other species. In spiders and dogs, the connections amongst brain cells are much more developed at birth than in humans. The dog is quickly up on its feet sniffing its environment, the spider is weaving its web. But with humans, although the raw materials are there, much has to develop.

While in the womb, the foetus's brain adds 250,000 new brain cells per minute during early development. At birth all the cells are present, but the establishment of millions of connections between cells will occur every second over the first few months. Also with development, the two hemispheres of the brain become more interconnected and specialised – a process that continues well into middle childhood. The baby's experiences of the world are essential to the structuring of the brain, which forms increasingly specialised pathways or networks to control different behaviours. The brain selects those patterns which turn out to be useful to the baby's behaviour. Between the brain and behaviour, the baby is progressively building up what are called 'mental representations'. This complex process gradually turns a brain into an individual mind.

The passage from automatic, reflex-like behaviour to purposeful, voluntary behaviour is of particular relevance to early development. This transition occurs as the part of the brain called the cerebral cortex progressively takes over the baby's behaviour from the subcortex. The subcortex is the more primitive part of the brain, most active during the first few weeks of life, and the one which controls all the baby's automatic reflexes. It is believed, for example, that the simple template for general face recognition is driven by the subcortex. By contrast, the analysis and recognition of individual faces is thought to be controlled by the cortex. The cortex becomes more predominant in regulating most of the baby's activities at about two months of age. This part of the brain is responsible for more voluntary behaviour and enables the baby to inhibit automatic responses.

It would be natural to assume that the initial underdevelopment of the brain is a huge handicap to the human species. In fact, this is not so. The early state of the brain gives humans a crucial advantage over other species because human brains remain far more 'plastic' or malleable in early development. Although the brain has some in-built structure, much of its subsequent structuring is deeply influenced by experience. If babies did not actively seek out stimulation, their brains might not develop normally. Compared to that of a baby human, a puppy's brain is far more developed at birth – even the bark of its particular breed is largely pre-programmed, constrained by differences in the vocal tract. By comparison, the human newborn

Far right: the baby doesn't just look passively at objects; he analyses the features and in that way restructures certain circuits in his brain.

brain lacks such rigid prestructuring. Paradoxically, because experience plays an important role, the brains of identical twins may not end up absolutely identical even though they start that way.

When the baby learns her mother tongue, say English, the particular sounds she acquires will cause the brain to link cells in a way that is slightly different from the way in which a Japanese baby's brain will start to link cells. Although they started with the same potential, the English and Japanese babies' brains will end up slightly different as far as the processing of language sounds is concerned. This is what makes it so difficult for adults to pronounce a foreign language correctly. Again, babies are smarter than adults. They can learn to speak two very different languages without a trace of an accent.

Even more interesting is the case of blindness or deafness. What happens when an area of the brain which is normally destined for input from the eyes or the ears receives no input? This is where the plasticity or malleability of the brain is important. A congenitally blind baby will develop a more sophisticated sense of touch than a sighted baby, although both start out with similar touch potential. And as the sense of touch develops, so the area of the brain normally devoted to touch increases in size for the blind baby, and the area of the brain normally devoted to sight decreases and/or is taken over by some other function.

Something similar happens in the case of congenitally deaf babies. The area of the brain normally receiving auditory input from spoken language may get taken over by visual input from sign language. This may seem odd, because in a hearing person one part of the brain is dedicated to processing auditory input from spoken language and in a deaf person a similar part of the brain may be used to process visual input from sign language. In both cases, however, it is language that is being processed. That is the common denominator. The fact that in one case sensory input from the ears is processed and in the other sensory input from the eyes attests to the brain's extraordinary plasticity.

The brain doesn't stop reorganising itself in infancy. We know that high-level skills such as reading reorganise the brain. And a post-mortem examination of a highly skilled musician's brain would probably reveal that more of the brain had specialised for music compared to the brain of a non-musician.

Not only does the human brain progressively gain structure, it also loses connections between cells. Pruning, or learning by elimination, means that each time a specialised circuit develops, another closely related one can be dropped. Cells that were somewhat active become inactive and can be taken over by other functions. To give an example: when Japanese adults learn English, they often have difficulty in distinguishing the letters 'l' and 'r' which their language doesn't distinguish. In other words, 'lake' and 'rake' sound different to the English ear and have different meanings. To the Japanese adult ear they sound similar. Early on, however, Japanese babies have no such problems with these sounds, because every single baby is born with the potential to learn any language. It is only as the brain circuits start to connect and the baby becomes increasingly accustomed to her mother tongue, that her capacity to distinguish 'l' and 'r' may disappear. In sum, as certain areas of the brain become inactive, these parts get taken over by other functions. From birth, the brain is a dynamically developing organ.

This all seems somewhat of a paradox. On the one hand, we believe that of all species we are the most developed, yet on the other we are initially the most helpless. We are born totally dependent on other humans, without whom we would perish. But because human babies are very protected, their brains can afford to be more plastic and open to development and reorganisation. In fact, initial helplessness is not only relevant to the plasticity of the brain, it also engages the baby in social interaction and learning from others. We are fundamentally social and cultural beings.

CONTROLLING PEOPLE

The ability to motivate other people to care for them is perhaps the most crucial skill with which babies are born. How would newborns survive without this skill? They are hopelessly ill-equipped to make their way alone in the world and must entice other humans – obviously, usually their parents – to protect them for a long period of time. Yet the baby accomplishes this rather well.

On the face of it, babies don't seem very sociable beings; they don't talk or smile, and they hardly even gurgle or coo to begin with. But they do have social skills of a sort, and parents are very receptive to them. It is now largely agreed that the baby's behaviour demonstrates a predisposition to socialise with other people.

Whether or not newborns actually intend to be social, or whether they just appear to be is a matter of some debate. The important thing is that they seem to be social, at least to their parents. This semblance of sociability greatly encourages the parents to care for their offspring. The baby's actions are frequently misinterpreted. The first smile may be simply a by-product of wind, but parents may

 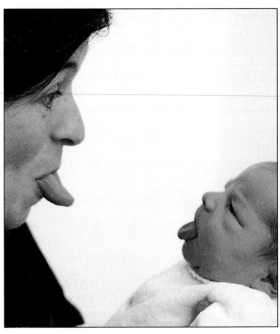

These two are not just rudely pulling their tongues at each other! This is a serious learning session in which the baby analyses what his mother is doing and imitates her, despite not being able to see what he himself is doing. This is an example of his growing self-awareness, which started in the womb.

interpret it as a smile and react accordingly. If babies act in a way that adults treat as social, then they are likely to become social with time. The diaries show how parents are quick to interpret any grimace as the social act of smiling:

> **Julia (three weeks):** I could swear she smiled for the first time today. I'd just finished nursing her and when she burped on my shoulder, I held her forward to look at her. This big smile came all over her face and I smiled back and then she fell asleep.

> **Xavier (three weeks):** Smiled properly when I tickled him and cooed to him.

> **Benji (five weeks):** I think Benji smiled at me today (this was Raj filling in the sheet today, but I've never seen Benji really smile yet).

Babies demonstrate early social leanings by imitating those around them. This is one of the most important ways by which they will learn about many facets of life during the oncoming months. The baby is born with an irrepressible instinct to learn and her ability to imitate other people is an excellent initial tool for this.

Imitation can be observed from a very young age. A newborn as young as one hour old will imitate adults' gestures. If the baby is held in front of her mother, and she pulls her tongue in and out, the baby will invariably move her tongue in and out in response. Experiments have demonstrated that movement is essential. A static tongue already protruded won't elicit the imitation in the newborn. When she imitates her mother's facial expressions, the baby is somehow managing to translate what she sees on her mother's face into similar actions on her own face, even though she can't see what her own face is doing. Recall what was said about the foetus. It was gradually becoming aware of the different parts of its body by exercising them in the womb. Perhaps this is what helps the later imitation skills. But even if it does, it is unlikely that newborns are conscious of the fact that they are copying when they imitate others. None the less, it is as if they were saying: here's something like me, and I can show that I recognise it by doing the same thing. And newborn imitation improves with time; the baby's tongue protrusion becomes more precise with practice. Imitation teaches babies what it feels like to be human. The diaries provide a clear example:

> **Dianne (three weeks):** She woke me up so many times last night that I was exhausted. The fourth night in a row. I feel like moving into a hotel! When I'd finished changing her nappy, I made the hugest yawn while I was leaning over her, and then Dianne started to open her mouth really wide too – as if copying me.

Some of the more recent research into infant imitation and memory has had quite startling results. The following experiment was conducted with eight-week old babies. A stranger peers into the cot and sticks his tongue out several times. Twenty-four hours later, the same person returns. Even though the second time the visitor remains expressionless, babies indicate they remember him by sticking out their tongues. By contrast, they do not stick out their tongues at a visitor they have not seen before, although he too remains with the same expressionless gaze. Sticking out their tongues at the known visitor is a way for babies to say: I remember this person so I'll do what he did last time.

Irrespective of whether babies are actually communicating when they imitate, the adult thinks they are. And that is what's important, just as the diaries show:

> **Julia (ten weeks):** Julia is really reacting now when we speak to her.

> **Evelyn (ten months):** It's quite clear that Evelyn has started to communicate more. She babbles back at us when we talk to her and she seems to answer my questions. If I say 'Are you hungry now?' she goes 'ababa' – really in reply. I'm sure she understands me.

The process of imitation often flows naturally into a communication game, a kind of conversation. So if, for example, the father coos at the baby and then hears the baby do the same thing, he will immediately respond by echoing the cooing. Or the baby may wiggle her legs, stay still when the mother starts making sounds, and then wiggle her legs again in response. A dialogue has begun.

> **Laura (seven weeks):** Laura is really attentive now when I'm changing her. She looks intently at my face and when I start chatting to her she makes all sorts of sounds back. I really have the impression she's trying to tell me something, like she has a language of her own. She's like a real little person.

These 'conversations' often occur during feeding. The rhythm of feeding between mother and baby initiates the infant into the basic rules of dialogue. All babies naturally suck in bursts, with pauses in between. The rate varies from baby to baby, but the pattern is basically the same. When the baby pauses for a moment, the mother instinctively fills in the gaps, jiggling the baby on her knee and talking to her. So the baby's natural behaviour – to pause when feeding – encourages another kind of 'conversation' with her mother and helps the baby's learning. Social interaction between baby and adult becomes increasingly intentional over the first two months of life. In fact, at around six weeks, if the parent responds to the baby's vocalisations with a blank face, the baby will frown or even cry, suggesting that she has begun to have expectations about imitation and social interaction.

If it's true that new babies are designed to respond to adults, then it's equally true that adults, especially parents, are designed to respond to babies. Much of the baby's behaviour is geared towards making parents react. Turn-taking and imitation are some ways, but another striking way is by crying.

A baby's cry is geared to controlling parental care. Initially, the baby's cry is just a reflex to pain, hunger or discomfort, but it reliably elicits parental attention. At the sound of any baby crying, a mother's heartbeat will increase and, if she is breastfeeding, she will automatically start to produce milk. By simply crying, babies ensure that all family life centres around their needs. Parents' reports show how babies hold families hostage to their cries:

> **Laura (four weeks):** The whole household is upside down since I had Laura. I never seem to have time for anything any more.

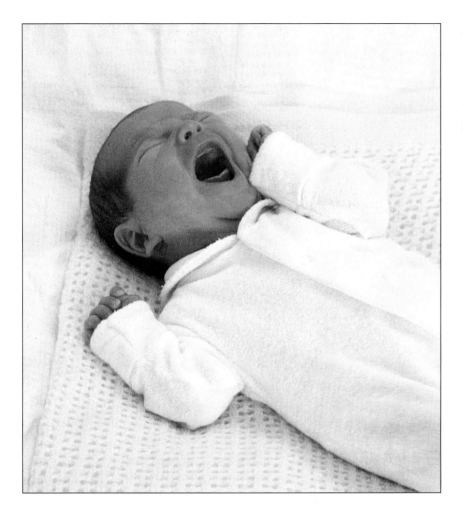

A baby's cry is geared towards controlling parental care. Initially it is merely a reflex to discomfort, but crying guarantees that adults will come to the rescue.

Just like imitation behaviour, babies' crying is taken to be a form of communication. Each time the baby cries, the mother will assume that she is trying to tell her something – I'm hungry, I'm in pain, I need changing, I want attention. When the baby is fed or comforted, she usually stops crying. This reinforces the parents' behaviour. Within just a few weeks babies build up expectations: if they cry, someone will pick them up. It has been suggested that this may be the baby's first understanding of cause and effect. Here is an example of this differentiated crying:

Morgan (eleven months): She has different cries which are quite easy to distinguish – sad, angry, tired.

At about six weeks babies add another trick to their repertoire: smiling. Like crying, smiling motivates care and attention from

The first smile may not be truly social but just a facial grimace. But once the baby notices the parental reaction to her smile, she builds up a link between this feeling in her facial muscles and the attention she gets from adults, and thus learns to give them genuine smiles.

others. At this stage, smiling may not be a truly social response, but more like a facial grimace. However, the reaction of parents is so strong that babies build a link between the feeling of their facial muscles smiling and the rapt attention they get when they pull a smiling face. This sets up a non-vicious circle: the more people attend to the baby, the more she smiles. The association is so strong that at this age babies will smile at any face at all – even a photograph.

Benji (ten weeks): He keeps smiling at the photo of his grandma though he still hasn't met her. She's arriving next week.

Sarah (four months): Sarah smiles at every stranger in the street. She seems quite indiscriminate with anyone who peers into her pram. It's lovely that she's so good-natured.

Adults ascribe friendly intentions to the smiling baby and begin to treat her more like a real person. She is on the exciting road to becoming a walking, tool-using, talking, thinking, social human being.

CHAPTER TWO

BECOMING MOBILE

The average human baby achieves in about twelve months what it has taken the human race millions of years of evolution to accomplish: the ability to turn the skeletal structure upright and move about freely on two legs. Yet unlike most other mammals, the human is born virtually helpless. Paradoxically, at birth babies hardly move at all and show very few signs of the efficient biped that they will eventually become.

During the first two months of life, babies start moving all the time and struggle to gain physical control over their own bodies after leaving the cramped space of the womb. They begin to uncurl from the foetal position and lengthen their hips when placed on their stomachs. If on their backs, babies will wriggle almost non-stop. These continual leg and arm movements are initially jerky and random. But they are not without purpose. However uncontrolled they may seem, the movements serve to progressively strengthen the baby's muscles. It is as if babies were doing a strenuous keep-fit session – which, in a sense, is exactly what they are doing. These 'workouts' will eventually allow them to begin to hold down their legs and arms, rather than keep them suspended in the air. The uncurling of the body and the progressive strengthening of the muscles are important as they give the baby more freedom to move. The diaries offer some examples of these work-outs:

Dianne (four weeks): When she's not crying, she wears herself out kicking her legs and arms around, hitting at the tips of the mobile above her cot.

Benji (five weeks): Benji hasn't stopped moving this morning. It tires me just watching him.

Laura (seven weeks): Laura seems to be moving her legs non-stop still, but in a more regular way.

The walking reflex **(from left to right)**. If the newborn baby is held just touching a surface, he will perform highly coordinated walking movements, with the left leg moving after the right and the hip, knee and ankle joints flexing and extending together. As we have noted, this is an ability he will lose over the first two months of life.

In most cases, learning to become mobile is composed of seven closely related steps: learning to hold the head up unassisted, to roll, to sit alone, to crawl, to stand alone, to cruise along by holding on to the furniture and, eventually, to walk. A small percentage of babies skips one of these steps; some babies never crawl or cruise. But most babies go through this pattern with little variation in the actual sequence although there is great variation in how they achieve it. It may seem strange to suggest that learning to lift their heads – something babies can't do at birth – is related to learning to walk. Yet these seemingly different skills are both part of the baby's drive to control the movements of her own body. And most importantly, every new milestone gives rise to a changing view of the world for the baby. The view she takes in on her back is very different from the one she gets with raised head on her stomach, and yet again different from the one she will achieve when crawling and eventually walking. In other words, the baby's drive to control her body leads to exciting

new views of the world, which in turn fuel the drive for more control. And these developments are accompanied by changes in the brain that make further developments possible. The strength and co-ordination that slowly develop result in increasingly specialised circuits in the brain, which in turn lead to more refined muscular control. A non-vicious circle!

THE WALKING REFLEX

In marked contrast to other mammals, human newborns seem woefully ill-equipped with the physical characteristics that will eventually enable them to move freely. Although the major bone structures are in place, the baby does not have a full set of bones in the hands, wrists, ankles and feet. All of the baby's bones are softer than an adult's, and although she is born with all the muscle fibres she will ever have, these too are small and weak. The baby also has a very thick layer of body fat which has been developing since week 34

As the walking reflex disappears, the young infant tends to make froglike movements, especially when on her back and in the bath.

in the womb, and which reaches a peak thickness at about nine months, before it is very gradually converted into muscle. As the diaries illustrate, parents are aware of these bodily changes:

> **Joanne (eight months):** Joanne is so fat, I sometimes worry she'll end up looking like my mother-in-law! The doctor assured me that this is puppy fat and that she'll slim down once she starts to walk.

> **Evelyn (thirteen months):** She looks a bit more like a human being now that she's lost that Michelin-tyre look!

Newborns, then, are floppy and uncoordinated, and still curled up in the foetal position after their stay in the womb. It would be natural to assume that the development of mobility proceeds from total helplessness through to the ability to walk unaided. Yet this is not so. In fact, a newborn baby is better at 'walking' than a five-month-old. Of course, newborns are virtually immobile – they cannot lift their heads or move their limbs in anything other than a jerky way. Yet they are born with an important reflex that is an index of the biped they will eventually become: the walking reflex.

At birth, if babies are held in the air or just touching a surface they spontaneously make movements that make them look as if they could already walk. Their legs will automatically press down and kick out. Even though they are totally unable to support their own weight, they can perform highly co-ordinated walking movements, with one leg moving after the other, and the hip, knee and ankle joints flexing and extending together. Yet a month later, babies seem to have lost the capacity they had at birth. At best, one-month-olds kick with one leg in a far less co-ordinated way. So at birth babies can do things that older infants cannot. Why is this?

The loss of ability seems to be due to an increase in the baby's weight, which at this stage is fat rather than muscle. Although many researchers explain the apparent loss of the walking reflex in terms of an increase in body weight and the slow development of muscle strength, some suggest that one important difference between the newborn and the two- to seven-month-old is that the older babies are much more interested in looking at their surroundings. This takes priority over demonstrating a reflex.

Even at five months, babies' walking movements are not like the alternating steps of the newborn. Held in the air or laid in a bath, five-month-olds kick both legs simultaneously like frogs. But by seven months, a lot of the baby's fat is beginning to turn to muscle. The constant workouts have paid off. Babies again control the joints of each leg separately, and if they are lifted just above a treadmill the pattern and timing of their movements are now better than the newborn's. In fact their movements look exactly like adult walking. All that they now need is the ability to support their own bodies. Here's a nice example from the diaries:

> **Goran (ten months):** He's not walking yet, but I've noticed that if you hold him firmly under his arms, he goes striking forward full speed.
> It's really funny to watch because he has such a serious look on his face.

When babies take their very first step at about a year old, this is often considered to be the very first sign of walking. In fact, it isn't. It is the result of a long developmental pattern involving both the maturation of the nervous system and the baby's constant activity. At birth, the walking reflex is under the control of the part of the brain called the subcortex which governs automatic behaviour. In other words, the newborn's movements are involuntary. Over the course of early development, the initial walking reflex together with the baby's constant movements progressively set up a pattern in the brain that serves later as a template for the toddler to start walking, once her muscle strength has increased enough to support her body alone. If one of the areas of the body had not been exercised at all – say the legs – then the part of the brain which normally controls leg movement would not take over that function and might be used for another. In the normal case, all the different limbs become progressively stronger as the baby actively participates in the structuring of her own brain. With development, what was the walking reflex increasingly comes under the control of the cortex, the part of the brain which makes purposeful behaviour possible. In other words, as activity in the cortex becomes more predominant, so the baby's movements become more and more voluntary.

CONTROLLING THE HEAD

At birth, babies cannot support the weight of the muscles, brain and skull at the top of their bodies. When newborns are held upright, the head flops uncontrollably unless supported by a hand cradled behind it. This flexibility is necessary if the foetus is to fit into the cramped space of the uterus.

A new view of the world emerges as the baby struggles to raise her disproportionately large head **(from left to right)**. Suddenly she can choose to look at things she couldn't see before. But the success is short-lived and she topples over, only to push herself up again.

It is hardly suprising that newborns can't move their heads. At birth, the head is one quarter of the length of the baby's entire body. Compare this with a fully grown adult, where the length of the head measures, on average, only one eighth of the body's total length. Imagine a six-foot man with a head that measured a foot and a half long! Babies' heads are disproportionately large simply because the human brain requires a lot of room. Other species of mammal like horses and dogs are born with smaller heads and larger bodies, because these animals need to be mobile from birth. As part of an evolutionary trade-off, the development of intelligence has made the human brain and head larger and the body smaller, to enable the foetus to pass through the narrow birth canal.

Before babies can gain control of their oversized heads, their bones and muscles have to develop and harden. For all babies, physical control and co-ordination begin with the head and, over the first year, work down the body through the arms, hands and back and on to the legs and feet. Obviously, then, babies can't learn to stand until they have learnt to sit. The process of bone-hardening starts from

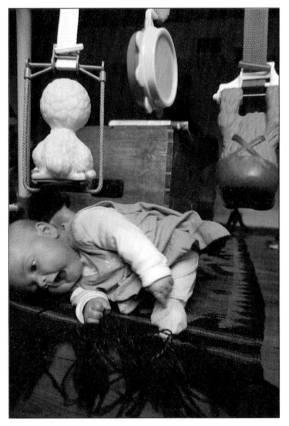

birth and continues through to puberty. It follows the same pattern as that of muscle hardening, co-ordination and control. All this proceeds from the head downwards and from the trunk of the body outward. This is why the head is the first part of the body over which the baby will gain control.

At about eight weeks, head and neck control begin. Instead of having the floppy neck of the newborn, two-month-olds can begin to support the weight of their heads by themselves. Examples from the developmental diaries illustrate this early period:

> **Xavier (two months):** Xavier holds his head almost upright on his own, though it's slightly wobbly.
>
> **(One week later):** He's showing more strength in his neck by pushing his head upright when held against my shoulder.
>
> **Sarah (three months):** Her favourite position is on her stomach lifting her head and chest off the carpet. Once she's in that position, she watches everything going on until she gets tired and then her head thumps to the floor. But it's soon up again. It somehow doesn't seem to hurt her, because she's so intent on looking at things. She even pulls her neck right round to watch me going in and out of the drawing room.
>
> **Lily (four and a half months):** There's a definite change here from the last time you saw her. Lily's trying to lift her head and shoulders away from the pillow if I've sat her propped against it. She loves me to hold her hands and pull her so her head lifts off the ground if she's lying flat.

Babies' drive to gain control of their heads can be seen in their continual practice at holding their head free of different supports. When lying on their stomachs, they will relentlessly lift their heads by some 45 degrees, for up to half a minute at a time. As they practise lifting their heads, the area of the brain that controls head movements begins to specialise further. Pushing up from the shoulders with their legs straight out behind gives babies – at least in tantalising glimpses – a new view of what's going on in the world around them. They may even push on their arms to lift their chests as well. And as soon as babies realise that they can see things differently, this will act as yet another stimulus for trying again. Here are some examples:

> **Benji (three-and-a-half months):** Benji looks so pleased with

himself when he pushes up on his stomach.

Sarah (four months): I put her on her stomach in the pram so she'd sleep while I was shopping, but she obviously likes the position, not for sleeping but for watching the world go by.

Margaret (five months): Now she's doing her 'push-ups', you can't do anything without her seeing. I was preparing a dinner party and spent all day in the kitchen so I put Margaret in the playpen on her stomach. I hoped she'd pop off, but instead she seemed to follow my every move.

For the very first time it is the baby who actually makes the world come into view. So by the time they reach about three months of age and have the ability to hold their heads securely, babies are no longer dependent on the whims of others to let them see the world. They can choose for themselves what they want to look at. This may be a small step for the adult observer perhaps, but it is a very significant one for the baby.

ROLLING

The next step towards moving around independently comes at about four months when babies start to roll, first from side to back, and then from back to side. A great deal of babies' energy goes into the frustrating task of trying to make their bodies obey them. Most of their waking time is spent moving their limbs and learning new rhythms. They gradually discover that they can make their legs do things for them – they can use them to remove covers or to make a baby-chair bounce. Rhythmic kicking like this is not play, but very determined work and, unlike the walking reflex of the newborn, this is intentional movement, driven by the cortex. The diaries provide examples of this more voluntary behaviour:

Sarah (four months): I'm worried Sarah will get cold at night – she keeps kicking her blanket off. She seems to have very strong legs now – maybe she'll turn out to be a marathon runner when she grows up – just like her aunt.

Dillon (five months): What he really likes doing these days is to sit in the baby chair and sort of bounce on his own – he kicks his legs quite hard and that makes it start to move.

When they start to roll, babies develop even finer control over their bodies. Some babies always roll in the same way, say, from right to

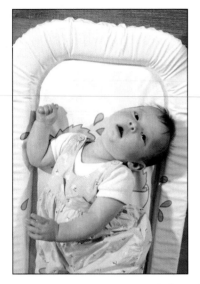 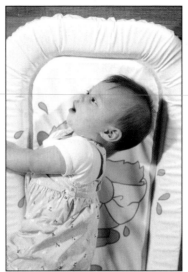 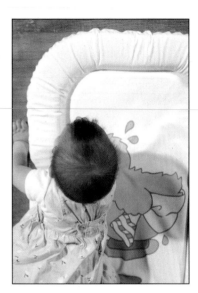

Another new view of the world becomes possible when the baby starts to roll **(above, left to right)**. At first she has no sense of danger and if mother weren't there she would soon topple over the edge. But just as the ability to raise her head gave her the chance to choose what to see, so rolling gives her the first opportunity to choose where to go.

left only. Others roll perpetually from side to side. Some will even roll right off their changing-mats and on to the floor. Later on, rolling is often used as a precursor to crawling, with their arms and legs held out straight, to propel the body from one end of the room to the other.

Like crawling, rolling is highly individual. Babies roll at different times and in idiosyncratic ways. Here are three examples from the developmental diaries:

Tommy (four and a half months): Tommy is lifting his legs and rolling to the side.

(**Three weeks later**): He can now roll in a circle.

(**After yet another two weeks**): Tommy can roll right over from stomach to back and back again and has started to stretch out for toys.

Amy (five months): Amy hardly ever lies still. When she's on the floor on her back (rare) she constantly waves her arms and legs about. She much prefers being on her front and will roll over immediately. This makes nappy or clothes-changing quite a struggle as she flips about so much.

Taffy (nine months): Taffy rarely rolls over and has never shown the slightest interest in crawling. She does, however, frantically move her legs in a 'sawing' action and can bottom-shuffle a little distance (like off her rug). Tuesday morning, I went to get her first thing to find Taffy on her front! She had rolled over twice before, at about four to five months, but nothing since. So I was most surprised. I think she was too!

It is important to realise that when babies first start to roll backwards and forwards on their changing-mats, they are not necessarily trying to reach a goal. They are rolling for the sake of rolling. With their repeated rolls, they are practising a new form of control, the mastery of a new movement of the body. But as with all the other movements, the baby will quickly learn that rolling gives rise to interesting results – namely, rolling changes the baby's view of the world. Once that discovery is made, rolling takes on a new function. It changes from practising at a new movement to aiming to get closer to coveted things. Whatever the danger, babies will now roll towards a desired toy, although they may often overshoot and roll past their goal.

By the time babies are rolling well, they still have to develop some other vital skills, such as a fear of falling. The three-foot drop at the edge of the table is initially no barrier! Without mother or father to catch them, they would roll straight over the edge in a kamikaze dive to the floor. Since rolling doesn't give babies a forward view, they can't see where they are going until they get there. Babies don't learn immediately from their mistakes, either. Even falling to the floor from the changing-mat doesn't give the baby of this age a wariness of going over the edge again next time. Indeed, were the baby to roll right off her mat, this would seem like an accident to the observer. But for the baby, it wouldn't be a mistake at all. This is precisely what she wanted to do! Although babies may have depth perception from birth, it is not until they are older that they learn that depths can be dangerous.

The difference is illustrated in these three developmental diary entries:

Sarah (four months): It's getting harder and harder to change Sarah's nappy recently. She keeps trying to roll over and I nearly had a heart attack yesterday. I turned to get the cotton wool and when I turned back, she wasn't on her mat any more! She'd fallen onto the carpet. She wasn't even crying, but I was. I was so frightened.

Evelyn (eleven months): Even when I leave the gate open Evy doesn't go down the stairs.

Ruth (fourteen months): When we went to Brighton, Ruth was on the edge near the beach but she was being careful, she didn't fall off.

SITTING

Before they can sit successfully, babies have to deal not only with the trial and error of finding the right balance, but also with the weightlifting exercise of pulling, pushing and levering their bodies upright. At roughly six months, most babies can balance in a seated position for a few seconds, especially if they are pulled up. But without some support, they quickly capsize. Some babies are placed

Sitting requires coordination and control. At first babies have to be placed in a sitting position by others, and they don't yet have the muscular strength and balance to remain seated for very long . . .

in a seated position at even younger ages, but they don't have the muscular strength to remain seated even when supported, as the developmental diaries show:

The slightest movement – even the shaking of a rattle – can upset the delicate balance.

> **Lily (three and a half months):** Lily can sit up if she's supported by cushions, but she often slouches and slides down the cushions which generally causes tears.

> **Dillon (six months):** Dillon seems to like it when I sit him up in his cot. But as soon as I turn my back he wavers over – he just can't seem to balance himself properly on his own yet.

Sitting is the obvious halfway position between lying and standing, and it is also half-way in terms of neuro-muscular control. As we've seen, the control of muscles, bones and co-ordination starts at the top of the human body and works downwards. In other words, after achieving control of the neck, babies have to wield control over their shoulders and upper backs, so that when they are held in a sitting position the only sag in their spines is at waist and hip levels.

As babies' sense of balance develops and the muscles in their backs strengthen, they become able to remain seated without support. They

Balancing when sitting is initially a complex problem. Some babies solve it by balancing themselves with the soles of their feet pressed together in the lotus position.

have to work out where their centre of gravity ought to be or they will topple over. Balancing themselves too far to one side will totally thwart their efforts to sit unaided. Usually babies find a solution to the gravity problem by placing their legs very widely apart. But another hurdle looms. Sometimes babies balance themselves by hunching forwards and supporting themselves with their hands, often keeping the soles of their feet pressed together as in a lotus position. These babies will quickly run into difficulties: as soon as they stretch towards a toy, they will topple over. Usually, though, most babies can sit unsupported by about nine to ten months. They can now even keep stable in their seated position whilst reaching for a toy. Here is an example from the parental diaries:

> **Joanne (eight months):** She can stay up on her own now for quite a long time – but only if she doesn't move her legs. This morning, after her bath, she had a toy in her hand – her favourite plastic duck – but when she dropped it and tried to get it, she went hurtling forward, fortunately without hurting herself at all. But she's a determined little miss and no sooner had I sat her up again than she was trying to reach something else.

Once the baby is really stable, keeping his feet apart to maintain balance, he can lean forward from a seated position to reach out for desired objects.

For some time, although babies manage to stay seated if helped by an adult, they can't actually get themselves into the sitting position. However, once they do, the cycle of movement expands: they can change from sitting to lying to crawling to sitting again. Babies' relation with the world again changes dramatically. For the first time, their hands are free to explore objects from an upright position.

Adults usually believe that the baby's first faltering steps are the greatest landmark in her early life. But for a baby, the simple act of sitting brings new and exciting powers.

CRAWLING

Strategies for crawling often arise by chance. During the process of trying to sit, babies may overtilt by mistake and use their hands to break the fall. They may then suddenly find themselves in a crawling position. This is obviously not a voluntary act and, still without the strength actually to crawl, the baby's legs remain entangled and trapped underneath her body. There are many peculiar positions that babies get into, as the developmental diaries amusingly illustrate:

> **Taffy (eight months):** When she lies on her back, she desperately tries to lift her head and legs up to try and get herself into a sitting position. We call it the 'stranded beetle' position.

There are other fortuitous movements that naturally lead to the crawling position. Levering themselves up on extended arms, as though doing a push-up, babies may start moving around in a circle, much to their own surprise. Some babies spend time rocking on all fours, and when they drop to the floor they realise that they have been propelled forward by chance. Other babies move about on their stomachs, 'commando-style', with their elbows dug into the carpet. Some even make swimming or flapping movements along the floor,

Through fortuitous movements while rolling and turning **(below)**, babies often manage to manoeuvre themselves on to all fours, and rather than going anywhere in particular, in the way an accomplished crawler would, often find themselves going round in circles **(opposite)**.

with their arms and legs flailing in the air. A nice example comes from the developmental diaries:

> **Amy (five months):** Amy's movement forward is an attempt at a hands-knees crawl, but it's very often two hands followed by two feet followed by a collapse on her front – a bit like a caterpillar inching along a leaf. On her front, she either looks as though she is swimming with her belly on the floor, or she does 'crawl practice' which includes being on her hands (held in fists, not flat) and knees then rocking back and forth. She also pushes with her feet. She sometimes even manages to 'bunny jump' forward a few inches.

Although by eight or nine months of age babies have developed the strength to stay on all fours without falling to the ground, all is not yet solved. Often their first attempts to move towards an enticing toy don't go quite as planned. Much to their frustration, they sometimes find themselves going backwards instead of forwards. 'Reverse crawling' is partly the result of babies' disproportionately heavy heads. Pushing on their arms, they tend to move backwards to get extra leverage. At this stage, babies' arms are stronger than their legs – the increase in muscular power and co-ordination is still working its way down the body. But the main problem is that crawling requires quite detailed planning: the baby has to learn which arm to raise with which leg. If she gets it wrong, she can suddenly find herself in reverse gear! Here's a nice example:

> **Margaret (eight months):** The funniest thing happened yesterday. Margaret was aiming for the chocolate cake on the trolley. She had a really determined look on her face as she got onto all fours. Then she kept sitting instead of crawling, until finally she went round in a circle and then started moving backwards – further away from the cake. It was so funny to watch her. I almost cried with laughter but she seemed frustrated.

The frustration of early attempts to crawl is usually short-lived. Babies manage to move forwards in the end. But they do so in very different ways – by bear-walking, rolling, humping, squirming, or bottom-shuffling. In contrast to learning to walk, where babies broadly follow the same developmental path, when it comes to crawling, some never do it at all, and most get around in highly individual ways – just as long as it is fast and reliable.

There is clearly more to crawling than imitation. Otherwise, why do babies learn to crawl in the first place? Crawling is not something that they copy from adults. In fact, it is an expression of the baby's insatiable drive to have greater mobility and increasing control over her body and her environment. She is now free to decide where she wants to explore and is no longer dependent on others to move her to her goals. And with greater mobility come greater intellectual demands. As the baby moves alone towards an object, she has to hold a goal in mind for longer than when she was immobile and things were brought to her.

The diaries show how varied children's development can be. Consider a cross-section of babies from the series: Sorsha never crawled at all but went straight from sitting to standing by pulling herself up on the furniture; Cameron and Theo both crawled forwards 'commando-style' at nine months. Most of the others crawled in a somewhat more conventional manner, at between eight and ten months of age.

> **Amy (six months):** Amy has a regular hands-and-knees crawling style almost all of the time. Sometimes she crawls on hands and feet, bear-style, especially when she is trying to go fast (such as when we play chase).

> **Sarah (six months):** She gets up onto all fours but doesn't yet seem to go anywhere – just flops down again.

> **Joanne (seven months):** Joanne never seems to tire of going up and down on her hands and knees but often only moves a bit, not really forwards.

> **Goran (ten months):** He seems to go forward now with alternate hands but somehow drags both legs together behind.

> **Morgan (ten months):** Morgan is crawling at great speed. But if she has an object, such as a crayon, in her hand, and she wants to crawl away, she puts it in her mouth and carries it like a dog.

What effect does becoming mobile have on the baby's understanding of the world? Does mobility in any way speed up intellectual development? These are questions raised by researchers who carried out an experiment using three groups of babies all aged eight and a half months, but at different stages of mobility. Babies in the first group were relatively immobile, not crawling at all. Babies in the second group were regularly put in baby-walkers, and those in the third were crawling on their hands and knees. Both of the mobile groups had been moving around for about nine weeks. The three

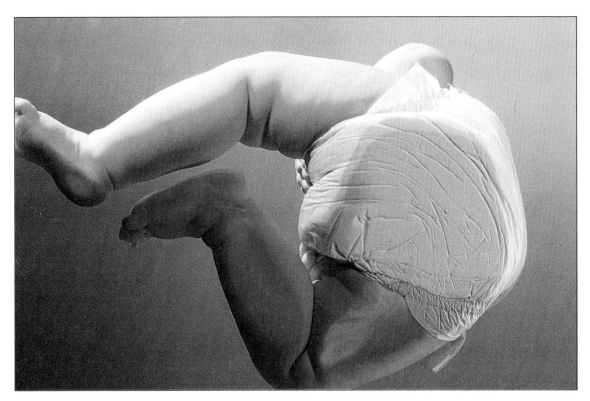

groups of babies were tested on three different tasks involving searching for toys hidden on the table in front of them. None of these tasks required the infant to move around the room at all. None the less, the results showed that the second and third groups, those who were mobile, did far better than the immobile babies at tracking the hidden toys, despite the fact that all three groups were exactly the same age. This result suggests that locomotion not only changes babies' view of the world but actually enhances their more general development by providing them with many different perspectives on their environment.

Crawling allows babies to move around rapidly. However, if they had the same lack of fear that they had when merely rolling, they would now be constantly exposed to danger. Fortunately, human beings have evolved in such a way that fear of depth emerges when it becomes essential for survival. Some two weeks after they start to move about freely – in other words, just when they need it the most – babies begin to show a fear of depth. For example, when a baby-gate has been left open, they may excitedly approach a flight of stairs and, instead of plummeting down head-first as they might have done only a couple of weeks earlier, they will now stop in their tracks as

Some babies never crawl but if they do they manage to find many idiosyncratic solutions: some get around on hands and knees (**left, above**), others go commando-style on hands and feet (**left, below**), some are very efficient bottom-shufflers (**above**). There is no standard method.

soon as they see the drop. We have already seen one example of this, but here are a couple more:

> **Ruth (fourteen-and-a-half months):** Ruth seems a bit scared of heights. We went out on the pier and she wouldn't go down the stairs with me – cried like a baby to be picked up and carried.

> **Evelyn (fifteen months):** She's much more in control of where she goes whether on all fours or walking. I really don't have to close the back door because the flight of steps into the garden acts as a deterrent. She goes up to the edge looking quite naughty, but then she frets because she's clearly scared to go down on her own.

Here are two accomplished crawlers going about their business. Although crawling will remain for a long time more efficient than walking, nevertheless these two will soon be attempting to pull themselves up on their feet.

A common experiment to test for the presence of fear of depth in crawlers is performed by placing the baby on a flat surface which is joined, at the same level, to a transparent perspex surface, creating a 'false cliff'. The mother stands on the far side of the perspex sheet and calls the baby over to her. A baby who has only just started to crawl will quite happily make her way across both the solid and the perspex surfaces to her mother. But after only two weeks of crawling experience, she will hesitate, fret and refuse to crawl across the

transparent part of the surface, despite her mother's calls. Thus, although perception of depth is innate, babies do not develop fear of depth until they are likely to be endangered by their own movements.

MAPPING

Once babies have mastered crawling, they are free to explore the world on their own. In a strange place, they carefully map out their surroundings and form mental images of the layout. If a baby is allowed to crawl freely in a café where her mother is enjoying a cup of coffee, she will endlessly explore the areas between the chairs and around and under the tables. In this way her mind gradually constructs a spatial map of the relative positions of objects and people in her surroundings, but always with mother as the focal point. She will make umpteen detours, even head for the door, moving further and further away from mother. But she will constantly come back to her starting point, as if she had an in-built homing device. So during her wanderings, she will continually glance back to check that her mother is still present, in the same place.

> **Cameron (ten and a half months)**: Cameron has become much more confident with exploring and will crawl out of the room I'm in and go off and play in the other rooms. Up until this week, I always had to be in his sight. He would only leave the room for a couple of seconds.

> **Leslie (fourteen months)**: She's become a real explorer. Took her the other day to my friend's house and though she'd never been there before, she went all over the place, opening cupboards – really nosey – and going in and out of the different rooms. She'd occasionally pop her head around the door, though, to see if we were still there, and then off she'd go again. Once she got her fingers caught, so then she bawled. Otherwise she seemed really happy.

The baby's drive to plot these spatial maps seems endless; she can cover up to a quarter of a mile in one session, going to and fro on her hands and knees. Exploration fuels the desire for more exploration. Initially, babies' mental maps of their environment are confined to those indicating how to get from, say, the kitchen to the living room at home. But as they build further mental maps of the different areas they are allowed to explore, the world expands from the confined spaces of their parents' home and becomes a more exciting place than it was just a few months earlier. As they start to piece together the

The baby's drive to explore his environment is endless. As he daringly maps out a new territory **(right, above)**, he may cover large distances on his own, even going as far as the door **(right, below)**, but always checking that mother is still there and frequently returning to her as if he had a built-in homing device **(opposite)**.

fragmented charts of their various explorations, mapping gives babies a growing sense of their place in the wider world.

STANDING AND CRUISING

Even though many babies can move around with great speed and efficiency as crawlers, their drive to get up on two legs is insatiable:

Taffy (eleven months): Finally! Taffy can now roll around from lying on her back and push herself up into a sitting position. Then she pulls herself up to a standing postion. I went to get her from a nap and there she was standing up and gripping on to the cot for dear life. I don't know who was more shocked!

Evelyn (eleven months): Evy's new trick is pulling herself up in the cot, in the playpen, anywhere she can. She can't actually walk or even really stand without holding on, but she seems to love to get herself up onto her two feet. She looks really funny sometimes, because a couple of times when she's started to pull herself up a bit too far away from the bars, she ends up leaning too far forwards and can't get up or down. She just half-stands there, rocking backwards and forwards.

The drive to become a biped is relentless: anything will serve to pull the baby up on his two feet.

Repeated practice at standing gives rise to the discovery that the baby can use familiar objects and landmarks to try out a new skill: cruising. Babies now have increased muscular strength and repeatedly struggle to haul themselves on to their feet. Once upright, however, they don't yet have the strength or balance to stand unaided. So the living-room sofa, the chairs, people, pets – indeed anything the right height – becomes a temporary Zimmer frame. Here's a nice example:

Theo (nine months): He pushes chairs around the room, and a couple of times has walked a few steps pushing his toy cart. He can edge his way along using the wall for support .... He can stand holding on with just one hand .... He pulls himself up on anything:furniture, people, walls, cupboards.

(**Two weeks later**): Theo is now cruising along the sofa, around the chairs, from one to another piece of furniture, etc.

But even when babies manage to pull themselves up easily, they will invariably go through a frustrating stage where they are left clinging on to a sofa or chair and unable to get down again. They swiftly discover that getting up and getting down are totally different abilities. To get back onto the floor babies will initially plop down without control and seem surprised. After a while, the baby learns that her bottom must stick out considerably before she attempts to descend to the floor. What an older child or adult takes so much for

The baby's view of the world changes again as he gets on to two feet and cruises along, using the furniture as a Zimmer frame. The problem will be to negotiate the gap at the end of the sofa; once he reaches it, he will revert to crawling rather than attempt to stagger across the gap.

granted turns out to be a painful learning process for the young baby. A couple of examples illustrate this even in older babies:

Oliver (twelve months): He's moving about a lot now but he still gets into difficulties. For example, when he gets up onto his feet he sometimes rocks as if he's undecided where he's going, but actually I think he wants to sit down again and doesn't know how. He has really hurt himself sometimes just trying to get back down on the floor.

Neil (thirteen and a half months): He moves quite competently these days, but I sometimes hear him crash down – he's not got the idea about sitting from standing.
    (Two weeks later): I think Neil has got the idea – he's protruding his bum properly to get back on the floor. He lands more softly now and doesn't look so surprised.

Not all babies cruise, but those who do usually start in the final months of the first year. After an initial period of not being able to sit down again alone or being stuck clutching the furniture, within two to three weeks babies progress to cruising sideways around the furniture. They initially use three points of balance (two feet and the chest, two feet and one arm, or two arms and one foot) to stop themselves from wavering. Later they get more ambitious and hold on with just two hands. A nice example comes from the developmental diaries:

Theo (nine months): Theo pulls himself up on anything: furniture, people, walls, cupboards. He can reach very high on tiptoes and now gets down again by dropping on to his bottom. He stands on the points of his toes like a ballet dancer and can edge his way along using the walls for support. He walks along the edge of the sofa and bed.

Compared with crawling, cruising can be a slow and cumbersome way of getting around, with some obvious pitfalls like the inconvenient gaps between the pieces of furniture that cruising babies need for support. They may cruise to the edge of a sofa and then face a seemingly huge gulf before the next solid object – a chair. They none the less launch themselves forward, fall, and then rapidly crawl across the gap. Although crawling is very efficient, a baby will relentlessly haul herself up again into the cruising position to continue her route. The drive to become a biped is so strong that the baby will persevere, despite all the drawbacks. Here's an illustration:

> **Evelyn (fourteen and a half months):** Today watching Evy reminded me of when I started skiing. I just kept falling all over the place and spent most of my time in the snow getting up and down rather than going anywhere – certainly not downhill! Evy looked just the same in the bedroom. She kept holding onto things, moving along a bit, falling down, getting up again, moving a bit further, falling off the end of the bed she was holding on to, then crawling a bit, then she got up again, held onto the cupboard, but that surface was too smooth and she couldn't really grip so she fell down again. But a minute later, she was on two feet again. It's exhausting just watching her.

When babies are cruising and holding on to objects to support themselves, their hands are no longer free. They must hold in check their desire to reach for and explore objects. The compensation, however, is that cruising again brings a different view of the world. When the head is held upright while crawling, eye height is about nine inches, but when babies are cruising their eye height is some twenty inches from the ground. Clearly they can see many things while cruising that they could not do while crawling. Cruising also gives babies the opportunity to let go of their supports and experience for a few precious seconds balancing on their two legs unaided. The baby is only a few days away from yet another milestone: walking.

WALKING

The baby is now ready to put to use the mental template built up from her initial walking reflex and from the experience of multiple forms of locomotion over the previous months. For parents, the baby's first, faltering steps are usually considered an event of unparalleled significance. But for the baby, the first steps are probably no more momentous than the first head raise, the first sit, the first crawl, the first cruise. Months of single-minded determination have taken the baby through each of these milestones and on to the next. However, the enthusiastic feedback babies get from their parents as they take one or two solo steps is a powerful encouragement to persevere. Here's a nice illustration from the developmental diaries:

> **Theo (eleven and a half months):** Theo just suddenly started

The urge to stand is constant but a helping hand is needed before the baby has the muscular strength to balance on his own two feet. Here an older sister comes to the rescue.

walking all over the place on Friday. Up until then, he had only been taking a few steps. On Friday morning, my mother and a friend came to see him walk, and when he did, they clapped and cheered so much I think it was a real encouragement to him. That afternoon, he just set off across the room and down the corridor.

The parental diaries show a fairly wide range (eleven to sixteen months) in the age at which the babies took their very first step unaided. Here are two examples, one of an early walker, one of a somewhat later walker:

Cameron (eleven months): Cameron was holding on to something and I said, 'Walk to Mummy!', and he came! Only one step at first, then three, then he fell towards me. The next day for the first time he tried walking without my saying, 'Walk to Mummy'. He decided just to take off and managed three definite steps. Until this week he hasn't really been happy walking and holding my hands (though this was no problem with his truck) but the same day he was suddenly interested. He even did a walk right across the room holding only one of my hands.

(One week later): He is becoming much more confident at walking and took a record fourteen steps today, although they were very small.

Goran (fifteen months): This was a really exciting day. Of course Goran has already been 'walking' – he could get around on two legs by holding my hands, or onto my dress or the furniture or something, but not really completely on his own. Then today he took off! He let go of the fridge and walked across the kitchen as if he'd never done anything else. I was so excited and he obviously sensed that – he kept looking at me. He went back and forth, a bit wobbly, so at times he grabbed the table legs, but mainly he was out there on his own. I couldn't wait for his father to get back, but by the evening he only took a couple of steps – probably too tired.

Finally on two feet! But the new walker has flat feet, stiff, splayed legs and a ducklike waddle, and it will be some time before she has the gait and rhythm of a true walker.

At this stage the physical act of walking needs a lot of refinement. Every two or three unsupported steps are punctuated by a crash as

87

This confident walker is celebrating the joy of being a biped. Nothing can now hold back his exploration of his environment.

the baby drops to the floor again. The joy of being upright is offset by the lack of speed and efficiency. Walking slows the baby down. By about twelve to fourteen months, most babies have achieved some form of efficient independent mobility, though this is not necessarily walking. 'Bottom shufflers', for example, are notoriously late walkers – sometimes as late as 30 months. This is because, although they may cruise and show other signs of becoming a biped, the speed with which they can crawl allows them rapidly to reach all their goals. But even for walkers, crawling remains for some time a more efficient means of locomotion than walking. So when babies actually want to get somewhere in a hurry, or when they are exhausted from the arduous work of practising being on two legs, they simply drop down on to all fours and scurry off! Here's a nice example:

> **Neil (thirteen months):** He always goes back to crawling when there's a problem. This morning he was getting around my bedroom on two legs and he heard the dog on the stairs. Instead of just going off to see it, he fell down onto his hands and knees first and crawled to the door.

Interestingly, research has shown that babies can actually select different means of locomotion for different ends. When faced with climbing down slopes of different degrees of incline, those who can already walk will not rely exclusively on walking. They will adapt their movements to the situation: slide backwards on their stomachs down the steepest incline, shuffle on their bottoms down the next steepest, crawl forwards down the next, and finally walk down the slope with the least incline. So babies are not just learning to become increasingly mobile, they are also learning to select the form of locomotion that is best suited to each particular goal. Young toddlers might do this by trial and error. Finding that walking is too dangerous on a given slope, they may slip down to crawling. But in older toddlers, such choices are made in advance – a sign of their growing planning capacities. They anticipate what the slope will be like and choose the most suitable form of locomotion at their disposal.

The sophistication to select and plan the best form of locomotion is of course not yet available to the one-year-old. Flat feet, stiff, splayed legs and a duck-like waddle are hardly tools for effective walking. But by about fifteen to eighteen months, walking becomes the baby's preferred means of getting around. By this time, her gait has improved and she is slowly learning the necessary skills for effective walking – steering, braking, reversing, speeding up and

Far left: after thirty-six determined months, the child has developed the considerable muscular strength to allow him to run, jump and change direction, and the coordination and balance necessary to kick a ball.

slowing down. She will start to clamber over and under furniture and experiment with moving her body in relation to other objects.

Even when the toddler has developed great confidence as a walker, there can still be unforeseen problems. The developmental diaries provide a couple of telling examples:

> **Marko (fifteen months):** We have just got back from a holiday in Greece. All the floors in the villa were shiny tiles and Marko slipped and hit his head hard twice after they had been washed and were still wet. After that, whenever he walks into a new room, he'll bend down and feel the floor. If it's wet, he will turn around and go somewhere else. If it's dry, he'll go in. It's very funny to watch him bend to wet-test every floor before he walks on it.

> **Trevor (23 months):** Sometimes Trevor runs around really confidently and seems very self-assured, then all of a sudden he goes all cautious – like when we went to a big store and the entrance was marble. He looked up at me nervously, got hold of my hand before he stepped off the pavement into the store.

But even though toddlers have developed the skill and strength for walking long distances, they still prefer to think of walking as a way of exploring the world, rather than as an effective means of getting from A to B. Toddlers will go from A to B via C, D and E, get distracted on the detours, and probably end up covering twice as much ground as they need to. But when they get tired, they expect to be picked up and carried home!

There's still a way to go before the toddler becomes a competent walker. Stairs present a particularly interesting challenge. Getting up stairs is easy enough, although this is initially managed only on all fours. But descending them is another problem. The solution many babies come up with is to turn around and slide down from side to side on their stomachs. As the diaries illustrate, babies each find their own idiosyncratic means of dealing with staircases:

> **Cameron (eleven months):** Cameron spent half an hour climbing up and down stairs. He goes down backwards by sticking his left leg out and feeling for the step below. For the first time this week he managed all the steps going down.

> **Leslie (fourteen months):** If there are some steps, Leslie tends to slither down a few steps on her stomach – she won't attempt staircases. But she's quite efficient on her stomach and seems to

control it with her hands and elbows on each step.

Jimmy (23 months): He really can walk downstairs now, but sometimes he'll do it sitting on each step just to be sure.

When toddlers start to walk upstairs instead of crawling up, they often use one foot to stabilise their bodies and the other, turned outwards, to lever their weight upwards. While doing this, both feet have to arrive on the same stair before the next stair can be attempted. When later able to walk downstairs, they will similarly use each step as a landing stage for both feet, before finally being able to alternate them – left foot on one step, right on the next – as an adult. This progression is quite slow, as the diaries illustrate:

> **Jimmy (24 months):** He has all sorts of ways of getting up and down staircases. If the steps are a bit steep, he may decide to use sitting and bumping down, but otherwise he walks, holding on tight to the bannister – he won't go down without a bannister alone – if not, he holds my hand. He still doesn't do one step at a time, but his legs are probably too short anyway. He stops on each step for a breather and then goes on to the next one. It can take him ages to get up and down but he refuses to be carried nowadays.

At about 18 to 24 months, toddlers start to demonstrate much more sophisticated variations on walking – running, stopping, reversing,

Stairs present the final challenge to the fledgling biped. Although a competent walker on the flat, he still uses each step as a landing for both feet before going on to the next step. It will be several more months before he can alternate, left on one step, right on the next.

side-stepping, and jumping. By this time their knees and ankles move flexibly. They can change direction with ease, even stopping to pick something up before continuing on their way. Again we witness the human drive to practise and perfect new skills:

> **Jimmy (23 months):** He's starting to run a bit and when he hears music he jumps about to the rhythm.

> **Polly (25 months):** Polly loves running. She appears sometimes to lag behind deliberately so she can respond to a request to 'hurry up', with a beaming arms-outstretched run.

> **Gillian (32 months):** Gilly has become a little athlete. She is always jumping and lately she has been trying to hop. She is still a bit uncoordinated so it isn't really hopping yet – sort of moving from one foot to the other with a little jump in between.

During the period between 24 to 30 months, other physical changes are also taking place. As balance and momentum develop, the toddler's gait goes from waddling with her legs wide apart to walking with her legs closer together. Toddlers become increasingly upright, and with this their body shape changes. Their legs get longer and less chubby, and the developing arches in their feet make them less flat-footed. As their metabolic rate increases, they slim down and muscle replaces fat.

By the age of two to two and a half years, children have mastered a sophisticated array of two-footed skills – walking up and down stairs, running, jumping, hopping, dancing, and even kicking a ball. And yet only a few months earlier, they could hardly lift their heads, let alone sit, crawl, stand or cruise. Over 30 months, we have witnessed the child's relentless determination to become a fully-fledged biped.

CHAPTER THREE

THE WORLD OF TOOLS

Imagine a world without tools. Adults use tools every single day: pencils, knives, toothbrushes, needles, brooms, shovels, buckets and sieves. Tools are extensions of our bodies and of our minds. A stick can be used to retrieve an object that is out of reach, thereby making our arms seem longer. A bucket helps us carry sand or water which would otherwise slip through our fingers. A lever can give us force to lift a heavy weight. A pen can help our memory work better, for example when we write down a shopping list. So tools act as a sort of intermediary between our limited selves and the world. Human technology has also given us a set of more sophisticated tools that increase still further the speed and strength of our capacities: food mixers, vacuum cleaners, sewing machines, electric drills, cranes, telephones, faxes, typewriters and computers.

In a world increasingly dominated by the use of tools, babies have to master numerous skills that adults simply take for granted. They have to learn about hand-eye co-ordination, and to reach, grasp and manipulate objects. They also have to recognise different objects as potential problem-solving instruments. All these skills are vital. Babies progress from merely grasping objects that they can't even release, to skilfully using a spoon, a knife, a toothbrush, a bucket and spade, a telephone or a remote-controlled toy. And they learn all of this in less than 36 months.

LEARNING ABOUT HANDS

A prerequisite for tool use is the ability to grasp an object. Adults follow a seemingly effortless procedure: look at the object, reach for it, and then grasp hold of it. But this actually requires a sophisticated set of skills. The brain has to calculate how far away an object is, at what height it is and whether it is to the left or the right. These calculations are sent to the muscles in the arms so that they extend in

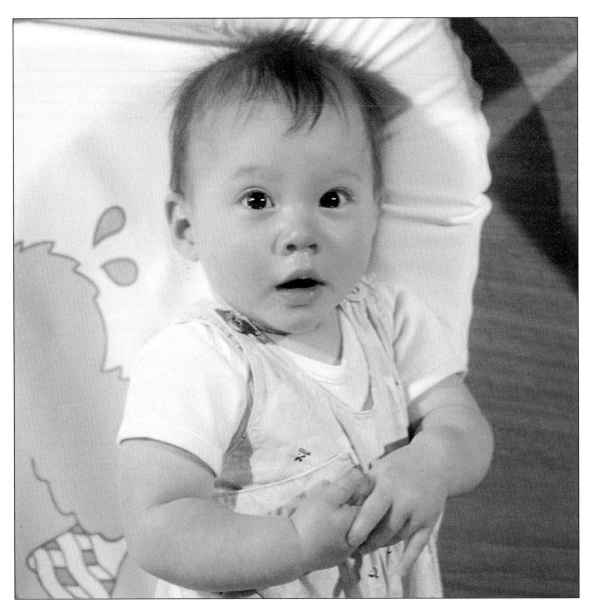

Whatever their age, babies are intensely interested in exploring their own hands. Their hands are the first thing they will grasp themselves, and this fascination will continue throughout the first year.

the right direction. And as the arms move, the brain simultaneously calculates what the fingers must do in order to adjust the grip to the size, shape, weight and texture of the object as the hand approaches. Looking, reaching, and grasping are perfectly coordinated in adult behaviour.

Babies don't start out with these skills. But how do they begin to acquire them when their arms and hands are weak and uncoordinated? Just as the future walker starts life with the walking reflex, so the future tool-user begins her days with the grasping reflex.

Although babies can tightly grip any small object placed in their hands, this is a very different behaviour from *purposeful* reaching and grasping. The abilities babies have to acquire are far more complex and follow an elaborate sequence of steps, the first of which is mastering the use of their hands.

During the first eight weeks of life, babies' hands uncurl from a tight fist. Among the first objects that they hold on to are, in fact, their own hands! Hands in themselves become something to explore rather than mere appendages to the body, and babies can often be seen lying on their backs intently studying their clasped hands. They also start to grasp objects like a mobile or a rattle when they touch them by chance. But at this stage, looking and reaching aren't yet properly coordinated. Babies may hold firmly on to an object without even trying to look at it. If anything, the object will go straight into their mouths. And they also won't reach for an object that they are staring at. As the vision and action pathways in the brain begin to develop, so looking and reaching become more co-ordinated. The developmental diaries illustrate this progression:

> **Xavier (nine weeks):** Xavier is studying his fist clenched and his arm outstretched. He holds both hands together in front of him.
> **(One week later):** He is now reaching out for things.

> **Rowena (four and a half months):** No overt signs of accurate coordination yet. Spends a lot of time still studying her hands and linking her fingers together.

> **Joanne (six months):** Joanne is now looking carefully at the things she wants to get hold of and manages rather well. She nearly pulled off my ear lobe by getting hold of my earring, and she also gets hold of my nose – that awful huge nose I inherited from my father! I just hope she doesn't grow up with it.

Just as they increase the strength in their legs by continually kicking them up in the air, babies build up the muscles in their arms and hands by constantly waving them around – a work-out for the *upper* body this time. Gradually, the jerky arm movements associated with the grasping reflex become more voluntary. This progression serves to consolidate cortical pathways in the baby's developing brain.

SWIPING

Swiping is the next step towards reaching for objects, but this is little more than grabbing in the direction of an object. Babies sometimes manage to hit the dangling toy that they are aiming for, although often they don't succeed. Yet despite their failures, swiping clearly reveals the baby's drive to make contact with objects in the outside world. And this drive is present from very early on, as the diaries show:

The baby may spend hours gazing at something he lacks the hand-eye coordination to grasp, or grasping at something he cannot purposefully bring into his own field of vision. Hand-eye coordination takes a long time to develop, but the baby will use this period to study the properties of objects he sees.

Laura (nine weeks): She's just beginning to swipe out at anything dangly – like my pendant, she's fascinated by it and always trying to get hold of it. Fortunately she usually fails, or if she does get hold of it by chance when I'm leaning over her changing her, then I have to prise it out of her fingers. She's got quite a grip.

Holly (two and a half months): This week she seems to be hitting the baby gym on purpose (that is, she watches the dangly bits before bashing them).

Lily (three and a half months): She reaches out to touch the things hanging on her baby gym.

Babies spend a lot of their time swiping at toys, and even accidental contact can teach them that their hands can make things happen. If the swiping is rewarded by a jingle or an interesting movement, this then encourages them to repeat their efforts. Babies start to realise that their own actions can have effects on the world, and in this way they learn which properties of objects can change and which properties always remain the same. It is an important learning stage.

Interestingly, babies seem to swipe only at objects that are within their reach. If a mobile is too far away, they don't attempt to hit at it. They behave as if there were an optimal 'swiping distance'. This distance may not include everything that is within reach, but it is usually reasonably accurate. This suggests that babies already have substantial knowledge of distance, as well as a sensitivity to the size, weight and shape of objects.

There are none the less a number of limitations to the baby's swiping behaviour. Although they may know where a mobile is located in relation to themselves, three-month-old babies still lack the coordination needed to reach and grasp it. The pathways in the brain for perception and action are different, and the former develop before the latter. One of the reasons why we know that these pathways are separate is that it is possible for one and not the other to be impaired following brain damage in adulthood. An adult with an impaired action pathway may know where an object is situated in relation to himself, but he may not be able to generate the action necessary to reach for it.

Another constraint on three-month-olds' grasping is that their arm muscles mature earlier than those in their hands. This is why their successful swiping rarely results in successful grasping. Yet despite these limitations, babies practise endlessly, even when their action causes them to miss a toy or succeed simply in knocking it further away.

Here are a couple of examples from parental notes:

Benji (three months): He is constantly trying to reach out for the mobile, but often keeps waving his arms at it without actually managing to touch it.

Sarah (five months): Sarah seems to have gone backwards. She used to grip things really tight, but now she bashes at things in the air and doesn't grab hold of them.

Any object is graspable: by grasping hold even of an unwanted object such as an onion, the baby will learn about the texture, size, weight and shape of new objects.

Once the baby can sit confidently, both his hands are free simultaneously to grasp and explore new objects.

REACHING AND GRASPING

Once babies succeed in working out the disparity between their hands and the objects they desire, grasping becomes voluntary. They now begin to grab at everything in sight, as the diaries illustrate:

> **Tommy (four months):** Tommy picked up his first thing this week (a rattle). He has discovered that he can grab hold of things such as flowers and hair. Anything within reach he grabs at. He sits on my lap up at the table and grabs at anything he can – including my dinner!

At about four months of age, when reaching and grasping first emerge, they form a single, amalgamated 'reach-grasp' action. As a result, babies may make contact with an object while reaching, but find to their frustration that their hands are tightly closed when they touch the object. What babies have to develop are separable abilities for reaching, touching, and grasping. These distinct abilities are fundamental for subsequent tool use.

Babies finally master the distinct arts of reaching and grasping at about six months of age, after which age the coordination of reaching and grasping becomes more or less automatic. Once the two actions are part of a properly-planned sequence, babies' skills can be extended to exciting new goals. Instead of grasping anything they happen to touch, babies are now able to push one object out of the way in order to reach for another. Here are a couple of examples:

> **Margaret (seven months):** Nothing is safe any more because she's learning to get at things even if I put something in front. We'd pushed the high chair close to the dining room table, but I may go back to the old system. I think there will be too many accidents.

> **Oliver (ten months):** Oli is into getting at things – particularly wine glasses for some reason. I put my plate in front of the one closest to him and he pushed it to get at the glass. Very clever thing to do, in my view.

But even at this stage, babies still haven't mastered every aspect of grasping. They continue to face the frustrating problem of purposefully letting go. When they grab an object, they keep holding on to it and can't let go until something else catches their attention, at which point they automatically let go. Learning *not* to grip an unwanted object is an important skill the baby has yet to perfect, as the following examples show:

> **Dillon (eight months):** Once he gets hold of something it's impossible to get it back.

> **Izzy (twelve months):** Doesn't seem to be able to put an object down. He tries though and drops it a few inches from the table.

At about the same time as they learn to reach and grasp, babies also learn to sit unaided. These simultaneous developments give them far more freedom to explore objects. Babies now confidently reach for objects with both hands, without the painstaking visual monitoring that was necessary just a few months earlier. They can lean forward to grasp objects out of reach, although their imperfect balance may sometimes cause them to topple over in the process.

These new grasping skills allow babies to learn much more about the nature of objects, and every object they explore teaches them something new. These explorations may sometimes lead to surprises – if, for example, they try to pick up a sunbeam, a shadow, a soap bubble, or a picture on the page of a book! Here are some nice examples:

Joanne (nine months): Today she made me laugh. The sun was coming in through the window so there were lots of bright bits and shadows on the dining room floor. She seemed to be stretching out for the shadows – as if they were real objects or something. Babies can be so interesting – I forget how much we know and they don't.

Theo (ten months): The first morning here (on holiday) Theo tried to catch the sunlight flooding through the window while I was changing his nappy.

Evelyn (twelve months): I was showing her a book full of lovely photos of flowers and she kept trying to pick them off the page – I couldn't work out if she was playing or if she really thought that they were real and she could actually touch them!

MOUTHING

Babies will put absolutely any object into their mouths – a rattle, a blanket, even the edge of a chair. They appear to be totally indiscriminate. The drive to mouth objects is rooted in the hand-to-mouth or Babinksy reflex. But the behaviour attached to this reflex develops significantly after birth, and from about four months mouthing is used purposefully as a means of exploration:

Tommy (three and a half months): Tommy chews everything at the moment. Possibly teething? He tends not to play with a rattle or toy – it just goes straight in his mouth.

Amy (five months): Amy continues to explore everything by putting objects in her mouth. She uses her mouth as a third hand to hold an object as she rotates it in her hand.

Sarah (five and a half months): Sarah sucks at everything she gets hold of – even huge objects. I get quite scared when she stuffs something quite pointed like a spoon into the back of her throat. But really anything – from the plastic lorry to the edge of her cot, she just sucks them all.

Dillon (six months): He is still putting most things directly into his mouth. Often he'll grab hold of something and doesn't even look what it is, it just goes straight into his mouth.

From the early months, when the nerve endings in the mouth are more sensitive than those in the fingers, the baby will use mouthing to explore objects. He will continue to use mouthing as a means of discovery for many months to come.

It might look as if mouthing were the baby's way of testing whether everything can be eaten. This is true, in a sense, but the purpose of mouthing is far more subtle.

To become effective tool-users, babies have to learn about the size, shape, weight and texture of the objects – not simply their suitability

There are no constraints on mouthing! Even huge toys will be explored for their size and shape (**above**). The baby is not attempting to eat the chair (**opposite**). She is using her mouth to send information about the features of an object to her brain.

for eating! To be able to explore objects fully, their two hands need to be coordinated, and babies haven't yet acquired this ability at four months. So their mouths become the privileged means by which they learn.

Babies' use of their mouths as an exploratory tool is a wise strategy, because at this age there are more nerve endings in the mouth than in the fingertips. The tongue, lips and mouth are amongst the first areas to develop in the cerebral cortex, and the most sensitive tools that the baby has for exploring objects. So putting everything in her mouth is the baby's way of learning more about the world.

Theo (nine months): Theo explores new objects by putting them in his mouth, by shaking them, by pulling, by swinging them.

Goran (ten months): I was worried about Goran putting everything straight into his mouth – things can be rather dirty. So I kept trying to pull them out and stop him. But he'd get angry and start to cry. Then one of my neighbours said she'd read that putting things in their mouths was the way babies could help themselves to calm down, so I tend to let him now. Though I do have to watch myself stopping him suck things all the time.

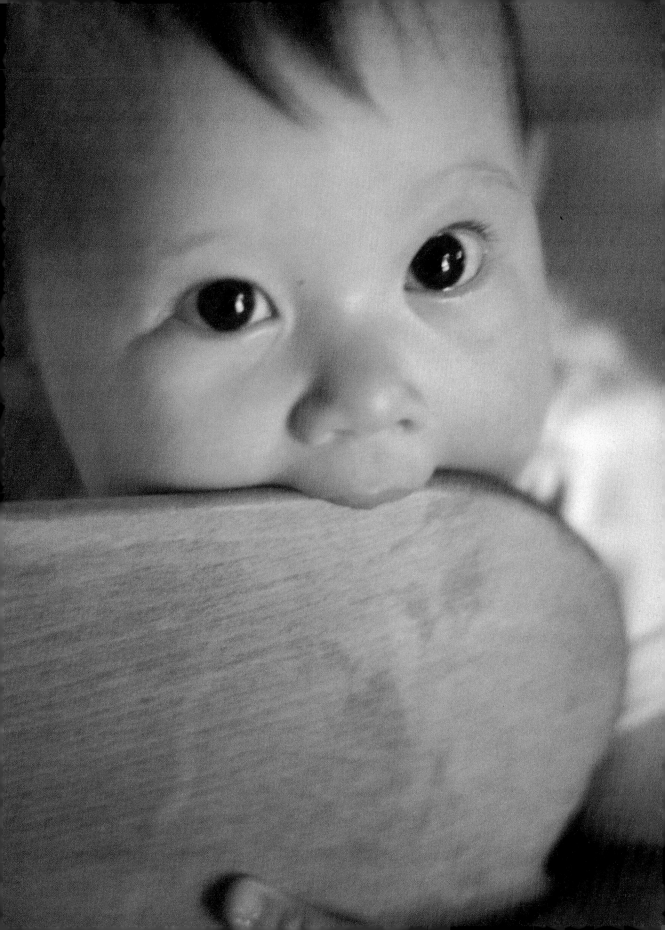

The most unlikely objects will be explored by the mouth. This is how the baby learns that silver-coloured substances are likely to be smooth and cold, and that objects can be made up of intersecting parts, such as the rods on a supermarket trolley.

Just how much information babies get from mouthing objects can be seen from the following experiment. Babies about two months old were divided into two groups. The first had a smooth dummy placed in their mouths; the second group received a knobbly, rough-textured dummy. Neither group saw the dummy before it was put in their mouths. While they were sucking, pictures of the two dummies came up on two screens. In both groups, the babies looked intently at the picture of the dummy that matched the one in their mouths, glancing only briefly at the other picture.

So the exploration of an object in their mouth enables babies to represent something about what it looks like: they can do what is called 'cross-modal matching' between what they feel and what they see. Recall the similar examples of the newborn's imitation of tongue protrusion discussed in Chapter 1, where we also saw that babies can imitate something that they can *see* on others but can only *feel* on their own faces.

So at this age the mouth is one of the baby's most efficient ways of learning about the world. Any mundane household object – a wooden spoon, a tin or an envelope – is something exciting to explore. Mouthing often continues well into the baby's second year:

> **Leslie (fifteen months):** She still has the habit of popping most things into her mouth. Maybe it's because I took the dummy away.

> **Jimmy (23 months):** You'd have thought he'd be over this by now but I still notice him sometimes putting new things into his mouth, not just things to eat.

It is only later when they can easily move around on their legs and use both hands in a co-ordinated fashion that babies start to explore objects by using touch and vision rather than by mouthing.

OBJECT PERMANENCE

Although reaching, grasping and mouthing are initially practised on objects that babies can see, they have yet to tackle grasping for objects that are not immediately in sight – a dropped toy or one obscured by a blanket. 'Object permanence' – the idea that things continue to exist when out of sight – is fundamental for adults. For us this is so basic an assumption that it is almost impossible to imagine a world in which this was not true. But does the baby share this assumption?

The baby's acquisition of object permanence is one of the most heavily researched and controversial areas in the field of developmental psychology. For many years it was argued that young babies think that when a rattle drops out of view, it ceases to exist. Object permanence was thought to develop relatively late, beginning at about eight months, and culminating between twelve and eighteen months. Recent experiments, however, suggest that some form of object permanence may be present in babies of six months, or even younger.

Imagine the following scenario. There's a short tunnel at the end of your garden and you enjoy watching trains go in one end and come out the other. One day, however, you learn that the centre of the tunnel has collapsed and that there is rubble on the tracks blocking the passage. You see a train approaching and expect it to stop. To your amazement it goes right through the tunnel and out the other side. Why are you surprised? The answer is obvious because you know that solid objects cannot pass through one another, and so the train ought to have been blocked by the rubble. Now imagine a similar scenario, but this time you learn that the rubble has fallen beside the track and not directly on top of it. In this case, you would not be surprised if a train went straight through the tunnel.

Something very similar to these scenarios was the basis of an experiment with two groups of six- and eight-month-old babies. They were shown a railway track with a small engine running along it. Instead of a tunnel, a short screen was placed between the baby and the track. They could see the engine start its journey on one side, briefly disappear behind the screen and reappear on the other side. The babies watched this event repeated many times until they got bored. At that point, the screen was removed briefly. One group of babies now saw the experimenter place a block on the track; the other group saw the experimenter put a block beside the track. The screen was then put back in place as before, so that the babies could only see the beginning and end of the track and not the part where the block was now situated. Would the babies anticipate that the block on the track would stop the engine, whereas the block beside the track would not? This is indeed what happened. Babies in the 'beside the track' group continued to be bored looking at the engine coming out from behind the screen, whereas the babies in the 'on the track' group suddenly renewed their interest and looked intently at the engine when it reappeared on the other side of the screen. It was as if the babies in the 'on the track' group were surprised. This suggests that they knew something about the fact that the toy blocking the track continued to exist even when it was hidden from view by the screen; it should have blocked the passage of the engine. Some form of object permanence underlies these babies' expectations. Experiments with infants as young as three to four months have shown similar findings.

There are some reports in the developmental diaries that also suggest that young babies are fascinated by object disappearance, particularly once they get to a stage when they can release objects on purpose:

Amy (five months): If Amy drops toys, she usually looks down and will pick them up if she is still interested in them. I have taped toys on to her high chair with string and she sometimes pulls the dropped toy up by the attached string, but this is often due to playing with the string itself, I think.

(**Two months later**): Amy always looks at objects she has dropped. She will sit down after standing to continue to play with a dropped toy. She also picks up food pieces which she remembers have dropped into the pouch of her feeding bib, if she runs out of what she's being fed.

Cameron (nine and a half months): He has a good look for a toy when he drops it. I give him a basket of toys when he's in his high chair and he picks them out one by one and drops them deliberately, then afterwards looks for them.

Theo (ten months): Theo now knows how to look for an object if I've hidden it. I put a bottle of water in our beach bag under some towels, so that he wouldn't find it, but he just kept pulling the towels out until he saw it.

Babies will often go through a stage of hurling everything on to the floor. Indeed, some don't tire of throwing objects until well into their second year. The parental diaries illustrate this throwing game:

Thomas (seven and a half months): Loves to play the game of throwing things onto the floor and then as soon as I retrieve it/them throws it back again.

Danielle (sixteen and a half months): Tonight while I was running the bath, Danielle picked up one of her shoes and threw it in the bath. I told her off as the shoe was saturated. As I was drying it off she picked up the other one and threw that in the bath as well. She still continues to throw things at the dog which she finds incredibly funny.

This is a stage of real experimentation. Once babies have perfected their skill at releasing objects, they will repeatedly throw objects, simply because they now know how to do so. By tossing things around, they make new discoveries. So they learn about the different sounds a saucepan lid, a biscuit tin and a sponge make hitting the floor. By the time babies can walk, they also experiment with putting all these new skills together – throwing something on the floor and then running over to pick it up, like a dog retrieving a ball.

THE PINCER GRASP

Towards the latter part of the first year, one of the most important developments for later tool use emerges. The baby starts to pick up

Babies will spend literally hours picking up tiny objects once they have mastered the sophistication of the uniquely human pincer grasp, which gives us a manual dexterity unmatched by any other species.

objects with her thumb and index finger. This is called the 'pincer grasp'. The diaries provide some examples:

Amy (eight months): Amy picks at things that stick up with her thumb and forefinger – e.g, corners of sellotape, labels on toys, my nipple when she is feeding!

Taffy (ten months): Taffy picks up many objects with great precision; she turns the pages of a book carefully and can lift the flaps in picture books with a precise pincer grasp.

Oscar (twelve months): Oscar has a very delicate grip of small items such as raisins on the floor and very precise movements when placing lids on containers or stacking objects.

The capacity to pick up objects with thumb and index finger is specific to humans. No other animal has this ability. An ape, for example, picks up things with its thumb and the whole of the rest of its hand. This gives apes far less dexterity than humans. You can easily experience this effect by tying an elastic band around your four fingers and trying to use a spoon or a screwdriver. Fine manual tasks are virtually impossible without the pincer grasp.

Babies are about a year old when they finally master the pincer grasp, which gives them the dexterity needed for sophisticated tool-use. They now seem to spend a great deal of time practising picking up minute objects. This activity is the basis for the later capacity for fastening buttons and small bottle tops, as well as for using pencils, pens and paintbrushes. In other words, the pincer grasp is an essential landmark on the road to becoming a competent tool-user – and, as the diaries show, one that toddlers continue to practise for a long time.

Gillian (33 months): Gilly's preferred activity these days is dressing herself. She spends hours getting the buttons done up, and usually sadly she's got the button in the wrong button hole so she has to keep starting again. But she simply won't let me help her. We've often gone out with her coat unevenly buttoned, but she's happy!

The toddler will spend hours emptying and filling containers, learning about the relationships between different objects and their sizes.

BRINGING TWO OBJECTS TOGETHER

A significant development that occurs at about the end of the first year marks another essential step towards competent tool use: the baby makes one object act upon another. She learns to hold an object in each hand, and then uses one to bang the other or to push the other from one location to another. This seemingly simple ability is a step forward, because now the baby doesn't merely use objects directly, but uses them as an intermediary between herself and the world.

Babies experiment relentlessly with this new skill, as the diaries illustrate:

> **Amy (eight months):** Amy has begun to hold two objects together in separate hands and bang them together. In fact, she bangs a lot of things to make a sound, e.g. spoons on tin, toy on coffee table.

> **Joanne (eight months):** She's started pushing everything on her high-chair table around. She moves the bowl with her spoon, and when she's finished eating she keeps the spoon and uses it to push all her toys around.

A natural extension of this new-found ability is babies' fascination with putting one object inside another. They quickly learn the significance of containers as tools to carry water, sand and small objects.

But babies are also interested in containers for other reasons. Containers help them discover how objects relate to one another. Given a saucepan or a bucket, babies will spend hours filling and emptying it with every object within reach. This fascination continues well into the baby's second year, as reports from the developmental diaries show:

> **Nicky (fifteen and a half months):** Nicky has an insatiable desire for new objects and grasps things all the time. He practises putting things into containers and taking them out again (such as paperclips into a small soap-bubble container)

> **Tanya (seventeen and a half months):** Tanya loves playing with Russian dolls. She is very good at putting together the individual dolls but hasn't quite got the hang of putting them inside each other yet!

THE ART OF FEEDING

Learning to feed themselves with a spoon is a complex problem for babies. Handling food with their fingers is so much easier. Yet like rapid crawlers who prefer to experiment with slow walking, babies will doggedly persist in trying to use a spoon. Their initial attempts at self-feeding are somewhat haphazard but indicate that they are learning that a spoon can act as an intermediary between themselves and the world. The parental diaries show that mastery may still be a long way off, but progress occurs daily:

Theo (ten months): Although Theo is hopeless with a spoon, he is happy to pick up and eat almost anything I put on his tray, and

Feeding involves many tools, which act as intermediaries between the baby and the world, and are the means by which the baby manipulates its surroundings. But coordinating the movements between hand and mouth can often misfire.

Hands can be messier but they get the job done.

The coordination required to get a spoonful of food into the mouth can be very demanding. But just as they insist on walking when crawling is more efficient, babies will persist in using cutlery even when feeding by hand is quicker and easier.

has no difficulty putting even crumbs into his mouth.

(One month later): The big breakthrough this week was that Theo has learnt how to feed himself with a spoon. He can put the spoon in his bowl, load it with food and then get it in his mouth. The mess is terrible, but he's getting better and better at it every day.

Cameron (ten-and-a-half months): Cameron managed to feed himself with a spoon, but only when it had chocolate ice-cream on it. He's not interested at all otherwise and throws the spoon on the floor.

(Two weeks later): We've had three more sucesses at Cameron feeding himself with a spoon – he'll only do it with yoghurt though!

Genevieve (nineteen months): Feeding herself is usually a combination of using a fork or spoon and finger with either hand.

For babies the coordination required merely to get a spoonful of cereal from bowl to mouth is very demanding. First they have to grip the spoon so as to get the food on to it. This alone may take several attempts. They must also avoid tipping the food off en route to the mouth. But much more is involved. The baby has to direct her arm, elbow, hand and spoon towards her mouth. If she fails to do this properly, the food will land on her cheek or in her hair. She also has to remember to open her lips at the right moment. Too late, and the food will encounter a closed mouth!

> **Leslie (fourteen months)**: Leslie gets over-excited. Sometimes she opens her mouth so wide ready to eat her ice cream, but then it takes her ages to get it onto her spoon, so by the time she manages it, she's closed her mouth and she spreads it all over her cheek. She's funny.

Feeding is a task that requires delicate planning and is often not mastered until babies are well into their second year. We've seen the difficulties babies face simply in learning to use a spoon. Learning to use a spoon and fork together is much trickier. And even when babies achieve this, they may still resort to using their fingers when the going gets hard, as the parental diaries show:

> **Nicky (fifteen and a half months)**: Nicky insists on using grown-up things to eat with, and he would rather struggle with a real fork than use a plastic baby spoon. Sometimes he uses his fingers to pick up bits of food though.

CREATIVE TOOL USE

Further skills necessary for successful tool use appear towards the beginning of the second year. Babies develop a greater understanding of the different functions of objects. They may attempt to brush their hair or their teeth, using the appropriate implements or even pretend objects: a spoon to pretend to comb hair or a pencil to brush teeth. Such actions don't mean that babies lack an understanding of what the objects are really for; the use of pretend objects simply reflects a strong desire to experiment with the functions of objects. Babies of this age may still come across tools that they cannot yet successfully use, such as a camera, a telephone or a hammer. None the less, their pretend behaviour shows that they have already developed the ability to invent strategies so that tools for one purpose can be used in innovative ways. The diaries provide some interesting examples:

> **Ruth (sixteen months)**: A lot of play now. She often just takes anything at hand and you hear her making noises and doing odd

Babies are fascinated by human artefacts and tools, even those they cannot yet use.

things. Yesterday she balanced the cat's plastic bowl on her head, saying something like 'raining, need dumbella'.

Kate (26 months): Kate tries balancing things and getting at things. Today she'd got the wooden spoon and spent a lot of time pushing down the back of the radiator with it. Afterwards I discovered that she had dropped a toy down the back of it.

The creative use of tools sets humans apart from other animals. Although chimpanzees use tools and are rather good at some forms of problem solving, it is rare to see them improvise with the functions of tools. Chimpanzees can be taught to eat with a spoon or to use a hammer to bang in a nail, but they would be unlikely to use a spoon as a temporary hammer if the hammer weren't available. What they learn well is the mapping between a particular tool and its particular function. By contrast, humans are creative tool-users. An adult in need of a screwdriver will improvise by using a nail file, a knife or a coin.

Babies improvise and invent, too. They may know that one object is particularly good for rolling along the floor, but they will also try banging it and pulling it, just to see what happens. Experimentation of this kind can lead to interesting results. A stick normally used to poke at things may help a baby discover that this is a tool that can also be used to get at something out of reach. As they experiment further with how objects relate to one another, babies may try to get at an object by pulling at whatever it is standing on. Here's an amusing example from the diaries:

> **Taffy (nine months):** We have decided Taffy is too clever for her own good! We placed a toy at the edge of her rug to encourage her to reach forward but she merely pulled the rug towards her, bringing the toy with it. She has demonstrated this more than once.

> **Goran (eleven months):** This morning my bracelet fell off my bed and underneath when Goran was playing on the floor next to me. He tried to crawl under the bed but he couldn't – he's too fat with his nappies and everything! Then to my amazement, he did something very clever. He got hold of the window stick – a sort of plastic thing that fell off the blinds – and nearly poked his own eye out with it, but then he pushed it under the bed. Of course, he pushed the bracelet further under, but still it was clever. Then I pushed something else under on purpose, but he didn't do it again. I suppose he had a kind of insight the first time but didn't really understand.

PLANNING

Planning is essential for efficient tool use. During the second half of the first year, babies start to make simple plans. We've just seen an example of how babies use rugs to pull toys towards them when they're out of reach. This behaviour requires thinking ahead and working out the relationship between the rug and the desired object. If the object is only partially on the rug, the plan may not work. But successful planning enhances babies' capacity to have control over their world. The parental diaries show how clever babies are at planning and using tools:

> **Theo (nine months):** Theo has learnt to move the basket we put in front of the video out of the way, and also how to remove the screen which is meant to prevent him from getting behind the television.

(**One month later**): Theo has worked out how to turn his
trolley around, how to manoeuvre it so that it doesn't bump into
walls etc. The funny thing is that he only seems to be able to turn
it in a clockwise direction!

(**Same month**): Theo has just started to be able to drink out of a
cup or beaker. Until recently he would choke, but now he has got
the hang of it.

Experimental data also exist showing how young babies become
quite sophisticated problem solvers towards the end of their first
year. Babies were shown two cloths, and an exciting toy was placed
on top of one of them. The toy itself was out of reach, but the
babies could reach a corner of both of the cloths. Without needing
any instructions, all the babies immediately tried to reach the toy.
Most babies under ten months old pulled on either of the cloths
indiscriminately and therefore often failed to get the toy. But by
about ten to twelve months, babies pulled only on the cloth that
would reward them with a toy. By eighteen months of age, babies
were also able to solve this toy-getting problem when three cloths
were involved. So some time during the first part of their second
year, toddlers can assess fairly complex situations, plan ahead an
appropriate action and thereby reach their goal. The
developmental diaries provide some nice examples of
accomplished planning:

Nicky (**fifteen and a half months**): This morning I put some
things up high in the hall and he wanted them, so he copied what
he's seen his sister Sasha do. He dragged a small kiddy chair into
the hall, clambered up on it and reached to get the thing he wanted.

Genevieve (**20 months**): After several amusing attempts at tilting a
cup backward, Genny learned how to drink from a straw –
without tipping the cup!

Max (**22 months**): He will go to great lengths to get something he
wants, that is, climb on a chair to reach the table to reach his bag to
open it and to get his container of biscuits to open it and get a biscuit.

Gillian (**33 months**): A real sign of intelligence today. She wanted
the paints we'd been playing with the day before, but I'd said no.
Then she got up on the washing stool, got hold of a spatula on the
worktop and tried swiping at the box where she'd remembered that
I'd put the paints. We nearly had a nasty accident.

Children are
sophisticated problem
solvers (**far left**).
Getting this desired
object required complex
planning from this
toddler: remembering
that an unseen object is
on the table; working
out what is needed to
increase his height; and
pulling out a suitable
chair to stand on.

An important feature of a baby's actions at this age is that she doesn't get distracted and lost in a 'sub-goal'. In other words, when she wants to get at a biscuit tin and has to go off to get a stool to stand on, she keeps her main goal – a biscuit – in mind and doesn't stop to play on the stool. The baby is developing an understanding of the relationship between goals and the different means or sub-goals required to reach them. Yet successful planning involves more than structured knowledge about means and goals. In addition, planning requires memory. Without memory, the baby wouldn't be able to hold her goal in mind in the first place.

Memory is of course relevant to all aspects of development, and it plays a vital role in planning and tool use. But how do researchers find out whether non-talking babies remember objects and events? A number of techniques have been invented for use with pre-linguistic infants, and researchers have demonstrated that a young baby's memory is very dependent on context – rather in the way that an adult's can sometimes be, when, for example, he fails to recognise his butcher when he meets him at the newsagent's.

In a typical experiment, two- to three-month-old babies are placed on their backs with a complex mobile hanging above their heads. Each baby has one ankle attached to the mobile with a satin ribbon. At first, it is only by chance that the babies wriggle the attached foot and find that this makes the mobile move. But once the babies discover the link between their feet and the mobile's movement, they start to jerk their feet constantly, intently watching the mobile move. If brought back into the same experimental conditions several weeks later (and in other experiments, up to two years later), babies will immediately jerk their feet. However, this time one ankle is not tied to the mobile. They show great surprise when the mobile doesn't move. By contrast, babies of the same age who did not have the previous experience lie in the cot without doing anything. The surprise shown by the first group of babies suggests that they remember the mobile and the effect their feet had upon it. However, if the experimental conditions are changed even slightly when they come back several weeks later – say, the objects on the mobile are a different colour or a different shape – then all babies, irrespective of whether they had the first experience or not, hardly move their feet at all. This finding indicates that babies' memory is very dependent on the details of the context in which an experience first occurred. Therefore it is perhaps not surprising that they may initially use a tool only in the context in which they first discovered it.

By the child's second birthday, and sometimes even before, her memory for the relations amongst objects has developed significantly. Once again, the parental diaries provide telling illustrations:

> **Theo (eleven months):** Theo is very interested in lids and tops to objects and tries very hard to put them on, twist them off, etc. Today when he found the top to a biro on the floor, he walked over to the table where we keep our pens, obviously looking for a pen to put the top onto.

> **Polly (25 months):** Polly has a good spatial memory and will remember the whereabouts of two halves of toys that have become separated, for example, carting a hammer from her bedroom downstairs to the kitchen in order the play the xylophone to which it belongs.

BECOMING A COMPETENT TOOL-USER

The formerly inept baby has now become a fairly accomplished tool-user. Toddlers can use their skills to achieve things that would have been impossible a year earlier. They can operate several household objects, like a telephone and a television remote control. Closed doors no longer thwart their eagerness to explore. They have learnt to open anything from a car door to a sliding door. Their exploration is constant, as the diaries illustrate:

> **Max (22 months):** He can open and close doors if the handles are the correct height. He's into keys and takes out keys and puts them in locks although he can't turn them properly. He likes to turn knobs, especially on the TV and stereo. He constantly presses buttons and knobs that operate the tape recorder, dimmer switches, etc.

> **Kate (24 months):** Her big thing is sliding the cabinet doors in the dining room – it makes me tremble for my glassware, but she really just seems interested in sliding doors open and closed. She's also into the TV – pushes all the buttons and seems to like the white noise non-channels the best!

By this time, toddlers have become so competent that they can now take on another important daily function: dressing and undressing. A toddler now has the dexterity not just to pull on her vest, socks or pants, but also to zip up a jacket. The seemingly simple task of

It takes intricate coordination to place a key in a small hole, turn the lock and pull down the handle to freedom. But the child will constantly set herself new challenges.

fastening buttons requires not just one but two sets of thumb and index fingers, so this still leads to frustration, as the diaries show:

Natasha (30 months): Natasha is beginning to master the art of dressing and undressing. She tugs at buttons in frustration and says, 'Mum, you do it.' Except I have noticed that when we go to our health club for a swim she will miraculously undress herself in super-quick time and climb into her swimsuit.

Polly (25 months): Dressing can take a large part of the day if Polly feels that it's 'Polly's turn to do everything'! She likes to do her own socks and is experimenting with some success on doing up the buckles on her shoes. She also likes to brush her hair and teeth (with the appropriate implements!).

Buttoning a cardigan requires a complex series of interrelated movements: the toddler must use the pincer grasp with each hand, while using one hand to hold the edge of the cardigan with the buttonhole, and the other to push the button through.

Brushing teeth is an example of how sophisticated the toddler has become at tool use. Like feeding, it needs careful choreography. Again the pincer grasp is relevant, but the toddler also needs to understand the nature of toothpaste – that it is neither really solid nor really liquid. And she has to learn to keep her head still when she moves the brush, rather than holding the brush still and moving her head! If she is brushing her teeth in the mirror, she has to take account of how her image is reversed. What seems like a simple task involves intricate planning and attention, as the diaries prove:

Evelyn (eleven months): Evy's into brushing her teeth – well brushing toothpaste into her hair would be a more accurate description. She insists on trying, so I put toothpaste onto her little brush and from there she's on her own – she wants to do the toothpaste herself but there I draw the line. She'd paint the bathroom with it.

Leslie (fifteen months): She now copies everything I do. I let her do her teeth with a proper brush but she usually manages to get half the paste on her nose and outside her mouth, not in it!

Jimmy (24 months): Toothbrushing is a really serious moment. He stares at himself in the mirror and often the paste drops off his brush when he's not looking. So I have to help him start again. He squeezes the tube but I hold on to it just in case. He's getting quite good at moving the brush along his teeth – I've shown him the up-and-down method, but he seems to prefer the to-and-fro method. But he often bites the brush which stops it moving along. The spitting out is the funniest part to watch.

A wide range of skills, such as using cutlery, fastening buttons, brushing teeth and opening doors, has all greatly increased the self-sufficiency and independence of the growing child.

TOOLS AS PART OF CULTURE AND HISTORY

If there is one thing that sets humans apart from other species it is our ability to leave a trace of our thoughts for other generations. Archaeologists react with excitement when they find a cave with ancient drawings or a tablet with ancient writing on it. We are all driven by a desire to leave some trace of ourselves behind. And young children are no exception. Take a look at any toddler playgroup and you will see many diligent little hands gripping pencils and attempting to leave their trace on paper.

But what do children of this age actually produce? Usually they are unrecognisable scribbles for the adult. But not for the child. Children are adamant that the scribbles on a page represent particular things – a house, a dog or a man. The parental diaries amusingly illustrate this phenomenon:

The human child is driven to leave a trace for other generations **(far right)**. However messy the final product may look to the observer, this child has clear intentions about what he is drawing.

Polly (27 months): Polly likes scribbling, especially on important documents! Her spontanous grip on the pencil is unorthodox but she accepts being shown a mature grip and maintains it.

(One month later): We do drawing together: Polly draws a circle and then says triumphantly, 'It's a cat!' She enjoys watching me write her name in large letters, naming the letters as they appear. (The naming is not consistent – she will sometimes call an O an 'egg'!)

Gillian (34 months): Gilly just loves to use crayons and paints. She's very serious about her drawings, although usually they don't look much like anything to me. Sometimes it's a bit like a person – at least there's a round part with a line coming out of it. But she's very diligent and can literally stay with one drawing for an hour or so, muttering to herself, in a world of her own. She's more expansive with paint. We've tried finger painting which is dreadfully messy – I prefer her to do that at nursery school. But with a brush, if I hold onto the paint pot, she actually does long lines quite artistically.

And even at this early stage, children do distinguish between drawing and writing. Experiments have shown that at two to three years of age, toddlers who are asked to mimick drawing will often make large movements, keeping their crayon down on the paper while they are drawing. By contrast, when they pretend to be writing, they tend to make smaller scribbles and keep lifting the crayon off the paper as they do so. In other words, they go about 'drawing' and 'writing' in very different ways, even if what finally ends up on the paper looks much the same to an adult.

So children are now learning another important aspect about the function of certain tools – that they can be used to leave a trace. Toddlers may not yet understand that the purpose of drawing and writing is to create representations of some kind, nor of course that these may be records both for ourselves and for the history of mankind. Even so, they have come an extraordinarily long way in just 36 months.

CHAPTER FOUR

THE WORLD OF WORDS

Language sets humans apart from the rest of the animal world. It gives us a way of communicating about events in the past, present, or future. It enables us to talk about things that are concrete and visible, like dogs and chairs, as well as about things that are abstract and invisible, like silence and justice. Just like physical tools, language extends our capacities. But unlike the ability to use tools, the competence to learn language appears to be uniquely human. Despite numerous attempts at teaching it to other species – from parrots to dolphins to apes – there is little evidence that any other species can acquire anything similar to the richness and complexity of human language.

Natural language has several distinguishing features. First, it is symbolic. Words stand for things. Second, it is arbitrary. The word 'dog', for example, looks nothing like an actual dog. And different languages say 'dog' in different ways. In French it is *'chien'*, in German *'Hund'*. So the relation between a word and what it stands for is arbitrary. Third, language is rule-bound. Each of the some 5,000 living human languages is governed by a different set of rules. Speakers of a language know these rules, even though they may not be able to state what they are. For example, English speakers know that the statement 'The cat eats the mouse' follows the rules for ordering words in English whereas 'Cat the mouse the eats' does not – although the latter does follow the rules for ordering words in some other languages. Finally, language is creative. When we use language, we are not simply repeating sentences that we've previously heard. Instead, we are constantly uttering and understanding sentences that we've never encountered before. To make the point, let's try one out on readers: 'The green dog who is eating this book is wearing a yellow silk hat.' It is highly unlikely that any reader has ever heard that exact sentence before, and yet we all understand it!

How do babies learn this complex system, their native tongue? We will again find ourselves faced with the striking fact that we've come across before: in some ways babies are smarter than adults. In fact, babies have a unique potential for learning language. Recent experiments have examined the ability of adult foreigners in the United States to acquire English as a second language, as measured by their ability to make subtle judgements about its grammar. They were asked whether sentences like 'The man puts on the table' and 'It was Peter that I gave the book to him' were good English or in some way odd. Although they had all been in the United States for a number of years, were all university graduates and spoke and understood English fluently, the results showed that the older the foreigners were when they had first learnt English, the less successful they were at making correct judgements. In fact, only those who had learnt English before the age of about ten or eleven years were likely to grasp all the subtleties of the grammar. So babies appear to be at a distinct advantage over adults when it comes to certain important aspects of language learning.

THE NEWBORN

While still in the womb, the foetus already starts to learn something about the language it will eventually master. For example, we saw in Chapter 1 that four-day-old babies can already distinguish the speech of their native language from that of other languages and that infants prefer to listen to a story they've repeatedly heard in the womb than to one they've never heard. This implies that learning takes place even before the baby is born. A newborn infant is also quickly able to identify the voice of her own mother, and prefers it to any other. The foetus's tendency to begin learning language before birth – even if it is only discovering the intonation of its native tongue – reveals that it is in some sense 'pre-set' to pay attention to linguistic structure. One mother reports on her baby's activity in the womb:

> **Dianne's mother (8 months pregnant):** Now I'm close to the end I'm very aware of the baby's state. It seems to move less now when I'm talking these days, but it starts moving more when I speak in Hebrew to my mother on the phone. It's as if it knows that the sounds I'm making then aren't the usual ones.

In fact, special pathways in the auditory cortex of newborn babies' brains are particularly sensitive to aspects of human language. Their brains are tuned to pick out the texture, pattern and rhythm of units

The two hidden eavesdroppers on this conversation are listening to the tone and pitch of their mothers' voices and learning to recognise the intonation patterns of their future mother tongue.

of language and to attend to these more than to anything else they hear. But while the ability to identify the overall patterns of their native language is impressive, babies still have an arduous task ahead of them: they must discover the formal rules that apply to their particular native tongue.

Although babies enter the world with a head start on picking out their native tongue from all others, it will take upwards of a year before they actually say their first word. This does not mean that the baby spends her first year idle; on the contrary, talking requires a number of skills that must be mastered during the first twelve months of life. The newborn's repertoire of noises consists mainly of cries and burps, but in order to talk she must learn to use her mouth and tongue to make speech sounds. The newborn's anatomy makes this a difficult task, because her voice box is inoperative at birth. Although this design feature makes talking impossible, it serves a vital function: it allows the baby to breathe and feed at the same time.

In any case, the inability to speak does not hinder babies' drive to become talkers. They practise the lip and tongue movements necessary for forming words well before they can talk. One parent observed this in her baby:

> **Benji (nine weeks):** Benji isn't really doing much in the way of making sounds (apart from crying!), but I have noticed that he moves his mouth a lot when he's in the cot or the pram. He pushes his lips forwards and backwards, like a pout, and then stretches them outwards almost as if he was smiling – but he does it like a rhythm, in and out and in again. He goes on like this for several minutes at a time.

It is as if babies were getting the feeling of what it's like to talk, even though their mouths are producing nothing but bubbles! But that is not all the baby is doing. As well as acquiring and refining the skills necessary to utter words, the baby is simultaneously gaining the ability to perceive and understand her native language.

Babies seem to be born with a crucial head start for perceiving the sounds of speech. First, from the moment they're born, babies hear speech sounds 'categorically'. If they didn't, they would think that people with different accents saying the same words were actually saying different words. Imagine how difficult it would be to understand speech if you didn't realise that the English 'my larst party' was the same as the American 'my lasst pardy'! The ability to perceive speech sounds categorically allows us to treat all the different pronunciations as equivalent. In babies, this ability allows them to segment the stream of speech into those sound units that matter for language.

A second important capacity with which the baby comes pre-equipped is the ability to discriminate amongst all the 150 speech sounds that can occur in any human language. In a sense, the baby is born 'international'. But before the end of the first year, this remarkable ability will disappear as the brain connections for categorising the speech sounds that do not appear in the baby's native language gradually die away. From that point on, learning to perceive new speech sounds will be difficult or even impossible. Notice what this means: an adult Spaniard learning English may have great difficulty distinguishing the sounds made by 'va' and 'ba', because the Spanish language treats the two sounds in the same way. However, as a newborn, this same Spaniard would have had no difficulty in discriminating between the two sounds. Once again, we see that in some ways babies are smarter than adults!

THE FIRST 'CONVERSATIONS'

Amongst the skills required to become a successful talker is knowing how to interact with other people – how to hold a conversation. Again, babies begin to learn about this process very early on, and by three months of age they are already using communicative gestures unique to our species. For example, the 'eyebrow flash' is an act of greeting used by humans throughout the world. If the mother raises her eyebrows, the baby will raise her eyebrows in return. Mother and baby thus begin to 'talk' to each other, taking turns, as in adult conversation. It is not clear whether it is the mother who directs most of this 'conversation', or whether she simply fills in gaps in the baby's movements and noises. But by treating their babies as valid participants in this activity, mothers draw them into the world of conversation. Here are two examples from the parental reports:

> **Laura (seven weeks):** Laura is more attentive now when I'm nursing her. She doesn't close her eyes but watches my face and holds tightly on to my thumb. Whenever she stops sucking, we have these little interchanges. She blows a few bubbles, I reply by blowing bubbles back and telling her how clever she is, and she watches my face all the time.

> **Benji (nine weeks):** He is frowning sometimes when he looks at me, as if he was trying to understand what I was saying.

By about two or three months of age, babies begin to make their first language-like sounds. These are a bit like the coos that doves make. At this point, babies have begun to develop control over the 100 different sets of muscles involved in making speech sounds. This musical, vowel-like 'cooing' is the result of their practice at moving their tongues up and down, backwards and forwards, and coordinating

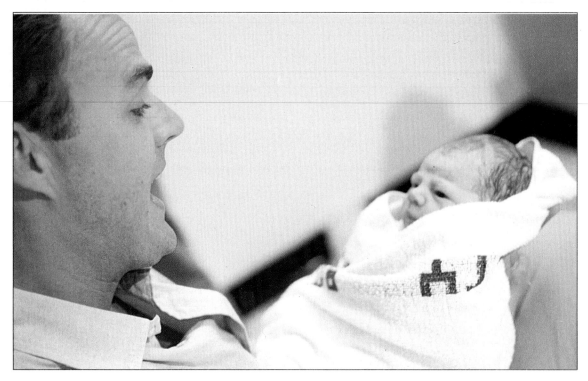

Fifteen minutes after birth and a dialogue has begun: the baby watches his father's mouth intently, and already begins to associate sounds with mouth shapes.

these movements whilst taking in air at the same time. The developmental diaries give the following examples:

Holly (two months): Holly does 'ahh', 'ehh', 'ahh-ahh' (high-low), 'oww'. Holly 'talks' much more now and copies shapes with her mouth even if no sound comes out. She wiggles her tongue around and 'talks' to herself in bed as well as when there are people around. She seems to like the sound of her own voice (must take after her father).

Lily (three months): Definitely more cooing. She has her own little conversations which are quite 'sing-songy' but fairly monotone. When I put her in the pram outside she chats away to the branches of the trees outside and then generally falls asleep.

The mother is likely to respond to her baby's 'coos' by cooing back. And when she speaks to her baby, she does so in a high-pitched tone and with simple, repetitive sentences that may sound patronising to adult ears. However, they are actually beneficial to babies. This special form of speech captures their attention and makes it easier for them to pick out the sounds from what they hear. In fact, this type of child-directed language or baby-talk has been given a special name:

'motherese'. While babies pay great attention to motherese, the mother's normal speech holds little interest for them. Few parents realise that they switch so automatically from normal speech to motherese, but one diary entry does bear witness to such self-awareness:

> **Evelyn (eleven months):** Still astonishing the way I find myself going from talking baby-talk to turning to a friend and talking like my real self. But it comes so naturally. Jonathan makes fun of me and when he imitates me I agree I sound really silly. He doesn't really do it as much as I do, but his voice does go a bit sing-songy when he's with Evy. All I can say is that Evy is much more alive when I talk baby-talk to her than if I try to talk normally which I have tried to do a couple of times. It sounds so pompous somehow.

Experiments have highlighted the special significance of motherese for young babies. In these experiments, babies are seated in a high chair, midway between two loudspeakers. The speaker on one side of

A few months after birth and the baby is already intently trying to connect what mother is doing with what she is saying.

the baby plays a recording of the mother's voice speaking in motherese, while the speaker on the other side simultaneously plays a recording of the same mother speaking in her normal voice. Although the speakers are playing recordings of the same voice, babies look much longer at the speaker emitting the motherese. This finding indicates that at this young age, they prefer listening to this simplified, exaggerated way of talking.

FROM BABBLING TO EARLY UNDERSTANDING

Only a few months later, babies make the next step towards becoming talkers. They begin to babble, repeating one syllable over and over again. You can often hear a baby in her cot repeating 'ba ba ba/ma ma ma' as if talking to herself. In fact, there is nothing communicative about this behaviour. Babies are simply working on a new skill, experimenting with the sounds they can make.

One of the most striking things about children's early language is

As the baby starts to narrow down the babbling sounds she makes to those relevant only to her mother tongue, she has to learn the right mouth shapes to produce the sounds she want. Here the baby is trying to say /eh/, the 'e' sound in the English word 'bed' .

that it is not always directed at communication. Babies seem to experiment with language much the way they experiment with objects. One researcher had a very clever idea about how to record this non-communicative play with language. She placed a tape recorder under the baby's cot and recorded everything the baby said when he was alone. She discovered that babies spend a lot of time trying out different sounds and different word combinations when they are lying in their cots alone. Other researchers have used the same method. They have recorded infants using long strings of experimentation with combinations of words like: 'My fall, mummy fall, fall mummy, teddy fall, doggy fall, fall doggy', followed by 'don't do it, don't doggy, don't mummy, don't teddy'. These are clearly without any communicative intention; they often occur in the dark when the baby is alone. They can also be detected in even younger babies when they are not yet producing words but sounds, as the diaries show:

Here she is trying to say /oo/, the vowel sounds in the English word 'moon'.

Here the baby is reproducing the /mm/, the consonant sound in the English word 'mama'.

Sara (5 and a half months): She's becoming more and more talkative - well she obviously can't talk - what I mean is that she's making lots of different sounds and she does this quite often when she's alone in her cot.

Joanne (8 months): Joanne seems to be fascinated these days with the sounds she can make. Sometimes I listen at her door before I go in to her in the mornings, and she's chattering away to herself! She makes noises like 'aba aba aba' etc. but she runs them together just like she were really saying something, going up and down just like in real speech. I wonder if she really is trying to say ' Mummy I'm ready for food' or whether she's just practising making a noise. Anyway, the minute she hears me, she starts to cry! So she must know that crying is the way she gets my attention.

Whatever their native language, all babies sound similar at this stage. They may even make speech sounds that do not occur in their own language, sounds they have never heard. So babbling obviously isn't learnt or copied; instead, babies simply seem to be predisposed to babble with the whole range of human sounds. Striking evidence in support of this claim is that babies born deaf – those who have never heard a speech sound in their lives – babble at first just like babies who can hear. Here are some examples from the developmental diaries of the babbling stage:

> **Cameron (nine months)**: He babbles tunefully, repeating syllables in strings (of at least four syllables), for example, 'ba', 'da', 'ma', 'na'. His most vocal time of day is when he wakes up. He's very vocal. He laughs, chuckles, and squeals aloud in play.

> **Taffy (ten months)**: Taffy now sleeps in until 7.30-8 a.m. Now when she awakes she babbles and chatters away to herself quite happily for half an hour. Brill!

> **Eiki (ten months)**: Eiki makes various babble sounds such as 'ma ma', 'na na', sometimes 'da da', 'ana ana', and click sounds, but he has not uttered an intelligible word yet.

Soon after babies start to babble – but still well before they utter their first words – they learn to use their eyes to communicate with people and to direct their attention. A baby will follow her mother's gaze, catch her attention and then move her eyes towards something she wants. This behaviour is common to all humans – something we do without even thinking. But for the baby at this age, learning to use and interpret eye gaze as a means of communication is an important advance, as the parental diaries show:

> **Joanne (eight months)**: Today I took Joanne with me to an exhibition in her pushchair. I noticed at one point that she looked across quite clearly at the picture I was staring at.

> **Theo (ten months)**: At the playground on Sunday, Eugene and I noticed Theo follow our pointed fingers with his eyes for the first time. We were pointing at pigeons.

> **Evelyn (eleven and a half months)**: We've both noticed that Evy stares at things she wants – often making a little noise. If we don't get it, she looks at one of us and then looks back at her toy.

Just before the end of the first year, babies acquire another useful tool for communicating: what is called 'declarative pointing'. Up until

Over: this baby exclaimes with delight, making the /ah/ sound of 'cat' when he sees an animal go by.

Here the baby's pointing is 'instrumental', in an attempt to tell his mother what he wants to have. Before the baby is able to speak, he can communicate by pointing.

now, their pointing has been purely instrumental – they point because they want something that they can't get for themselves. But now pointing also takes on a new function. A baby will point not because she needs something, but simply to share an experience with her parent. The developmental diaries provide a particularly nice contrast between these two functions of pointing. The first two children below are pointing instrumentally, whereas the last two are using pointing declaratively:

Oscar (twelve months): He's using 'yeah' all the time to indicate he wants something along with pointing at it. If he doesn't get the message across he screams blue murder!

Marko (thirteen months): Lately he points to everything. He seems to have just figured out that his juice and milk are in the fridge and he'll walk to it and point and shout 'Aaaaaah'! When I open it, he points to what he wants. It's so much easier now to figure out what he would like.

Leslie (fifteen months): She now spends her time pointing out everything we pass when she's in the pushchair.

Danielle (nineteen months): If she sees a bird in a book, she'll point to it and then point outside in the garden. If she sees a shoe, she'll lift her leg to show me that it goes on her foot.

It is quite clear that pointing can now be used to communicate with others. In experiments, babies have been observed with their mothers

Here the child is not asking for anything. His pointing is 'declarative': he is drawing attention to the light he has managed to switch on.

when an exciting new toy, like an electric car, passes by. A baby of this age will point repeatedly at the car, constantly checking that her mother is watching. This pointing is obviously aimed at communicating, because when babies are left alone and another exciting toy goes by, they look at it but they don't point at all.

Only a month or two later, although babies are still babbling, they practise their babbles in a more conversational way. It is as if they are starting to experiment with talking – without worrying too much about saying anything intelligible! The baby's babbles have developed into a much more speech-like form. However, this 'language' is a bit like a tune with no words. The parental diaries give an example of this advanced form of babbling:

Theo (eleven months): Theo has started talking in a very funny language of his own. It is very hard to transcribe but I'll try – 'Agalalaglaga' or 'Glaglagla', over and over again, very fast. It makes everyone laugh and he seems to enjoy it a lot.

(**Same week**): Theo now makes a whole range of conversation-like babblings, most of which sound like Arabic.

Oscar (twelve months): His 'nonsense' chattering has got more sophisticated and expressive. He's started having 'conversations' with other babies.

(**Same week**): Lots of talking in own gobbledygook, but with intonation and emphasis which are more like adult speech. Quite sophisticated copying of adult behaviour like pressing speaker phone button on telephone and 'talking' into speaker.

At this point, babies no longer all babble in the same way. Whereas only a few months earlier the babbles of an English and a Russian baby would have been indistinguishable from one another, the two babblers now sound very different. Deaf babies also stop babbling around this age as they start to learn the special manual gestures of sign language[1]. From this point on, hearing babies make only the sounds that exist in their native language. This type of speech is sometimes called 'shaped babbling' or 'scribble talk'. In this type of talk, babies produce long strings of different syllables, with an intonation that rises and falls just as in normal speech. They sound as if they are really speaking but in a language we don't know. This

---

1 Note that the world's different sign languages all have the distinguishing features of human language that were outlined at the beginning of this chapter: they are symbolic, the relation between word-signs and their referents is arbitrary, they have rule-bound grammars, and they are creative. Each sign language is different from the others. So although English and American spoken languages are very similar, British Sign Language is not the same as American Sign Language. Each one is a language in its own right.

speech is clearly more communicative than their earlier babbling. No longer is the baby just practising making sounds; instead, the intonation of her speech seems to carry some meaning. For example, 'aba aba bee aba bee ma ma' with a falling intonation may require no response, but the same string uttered with a rising intonation may make it sound as if the baby is asking a question and expecting an answer! And parents readily interpret their baby's gibberish by responding with comments like: 'So you want to be picked up, do you?' or 'So you're hungry, are you?'! Here's an example from the diaries:

> **Oscar (twelve months):** He adds to the meaning of his utterances with an increasing range of increasingly subtle and 'knowing' facial expressions.

Although babies have yet to say their first real word, they understand far more than they can say. This advantage of understanding over speaking will characterise the baby's language throughout toddlerhood. It is easy to see that babies understand when they respond to simple sentences and commands. And at this point they probably know about a hundred words, without being able to say even one!

As babies become more skilled at understanding and communicating, they no longer only attend to motherese. They also become fascinated with other people's talk. Even though they may not be able to understand much of what is being said in a conversation, they pay careful attention to the speakers, possibly picking out the odd word that they recognise. This diary entry is a typical example:

> **Neil (fourteen months):** I organised a tea party for some friends visiting from Scotland on Saturday. Everyone was really animated because we hadn't seen each other for a long time. At one point I noticed Neil was watching everything going on and he would occasionally pipe up with a word someone had just said, as if he was part of the conversation too. I think he liked the animation and listening to us chatting. Later that day he kept saying a new word – 'gago gago' – but we couldn't work out what he was on about.

There's a reason why attention to adult conversation is useful at this stage – it teaches babies more about the way in which words are put together into sentences, about the grammar of their language.

FIRST WORDS

'A word in your ear, mate'? No – at this age there is little linguistic communication between young babies and the children in this picture are simply playing beside each other and making noises to themselves.

A year's hard work finally results in the baby's first proper word. This typically happens at about twelve months of age. But even though parents are often delighted, they may also feel frustrated when their babies seem to limit their use of new words to special contexts only. This suggests that the baby has not yet learnt the adult meanings of the words she uses. For example, a baby may use the word 'car' when she is looking at a passing car through the living-room window, but not use the word 'car' when she is playing outside and sees the same car pass by. She might even use the word 'car' when she's at the window and something other than a car passes by. What then does the baby think the word 'car' means? Usually babies have initially learnt a word like 'car' in a particular situation, such as looking

The naming game: mother and child will spend hours naming objects. Young babies will extend a new name such as 'onion' to all similar round objects for quite some time.

through the living room window. So perhaps the baby thinks 'car' means something like 'me-looking-through-the-window-at-passing-things'! The diaries provide a couple of examples:

Joshua (sixteen months): Joshua knows the word for peas because he likes eating them, but when we were in the health shop today he made his funny 'ugh ugh' when pointing at peas as if he wanted to know their name.

Jimmy (23 months): Jimmy only calls his American toy 'truck' – all the others are 'lorries'.

This baby has a long way before he can use strings of words to get his father to do what he wants, so a good tug in the right direction will fill the linguistic gaps.

Some researchers have suggested that twelve-month-olds have yet to reach the so-called 'nominal insight', the knowledge that the word 'car' – and all other nouns – refer to objects across every context and situation, not just in a single particular one. In fact, it is difficult to know for certain what babies mean when they use particular words without also testing their understanding of a new word. Many of the baby's early words may not have the same meaning for her as they do for adults.

Over the next several months, word learning progresses very slowly compared to later on. Babies will learn to produce new words at a rate of only a handful per month. The majority of their words will be words for people and things, usually proper names (like 'Billy') and nouns (like 'car'). A baby's pronunciation of these words will often not sound exactly like it should in the adult language. If a word has more than one syllable, a baby will often pick up the stressed syllables before the unstressed ones, and so may call a giraffe, 'raffe', or an elephant, 'e-phant'. This tendency to pick up on stressed syllables is characteristic of babies' speech all over the world. Here are two examples from the diaries:

Eiki (thirteen months): Eiki says 'nana' for banana. This could be his first word.

Leslie (fourteen months): Four new words since I last filled this in: ca=carpet, ock=dog, o-o=orange, and ann=Suzanne. She seems to be paying a lot of attention to us when we're speaking now.

Later still, as more syllables are included in what toddlers say, their pronunciation may still not be adult-like, as the diaries show:

Ruth (fifteen and a half months): Ruth makes us all laugh when she tries to say 'puzzle' – it comes out as 'puggall'.

Genevieve (20 months): It was pouring with rain. Genevieve insisted that she and I go out for a walk. Anyway I took her to the window and pointed out the raindrops hitting the puddles. I told her it was cold and we'd get all wet. In my case for staying indoors, there was one thing I hadn't considered. So Genny piped up: 'Blum-de-bah! Blum-de-bah!' Unfortunately I couldn't reply with the obvious solution of using an 'umbrella'!

Kate (24 months): She still can't say 'string' – just calls it 'ting'.

As noted earlier, babies understand far more than they say at every point in the course of language development. Indeed, the baby can understand many words before being able to say a single one. This is not true of words only. It's even true for whole sentences. By the time babies are producing single-word speech, there is good evidence that they understand long sentences. In some recent experiments, seventeen-month-old babies heard a sentence such as 'Minnie Mouse pushes Mickey Mouse' on a loudspeaker positioned between two video screens. One of the video screens did show Minnie pushing Mickey, but the other screen showed the opposite action – Mickey pushing Minnie. Although the actions on both screens were potentially interesting for the babies, they in fact looked intently only at the screen matching the sentence they heard. This suggests that babies understand a lot about sentences and word order well before they can say more than single words:

Joshua (nineteen months): We all have the impression that Joshua is beginning to understand quite a lot when we talk to him – even when we use quite long sentences. But his language is still rather primitive.

Another important fact about this stage of development is that babies point continually. An important by-product of this tendency to point is that it will often lead the parent to name the object the baby points at. This helps the baby to learn that every object has a name or a word associated with it. By pointing at several objects of the same type and hearing the same word each time, the baby can also discover that certain words refer not just to one object but to a whole class or category of objects. Unlike the younger child who restricts words to particular situations, children now begin to extend the words to all their appropriate uses:

> **Genevieve (nineteen months):** She has lately been saying 'car' very distinctly as soon as she sees any one, anywhere, real or in an image.

> **Jimmy (25 months):** Says 'lorry' to all lorries now.

But this pointing-and-naming game wouldn't be a success unless baby and parent shared an important mental assumption. Imagine being in a foreign country, where someone points to an object and says a strange word. How do you know what the word stands for? Without being told, you automatically assume that the word stands for the whole object, and not just for one of its parts or one of its properties, like its colour. And babies appear to do the same thing because they share with adults the hypothesis that a new word always refers to a whole object.

Babies not only pay careful attention to the words their parents say, they also have a remarkably sophisticated ability to use their parents' non-verbal cues to help them determine what new words mean. Researchers have asked mothers to wait until their babies are engrossed in examining an exciting new toy, and then to look themselves at another toy and say a new word. An eighteen-month-old will not take it that her mother's word refers to the new toy she is playing with. Instead, as soon as her mother says a word, she looks up at her, checks where she is looking, and takes the word to refer to whatever she is looking at. Babies can apparently exploit their mothers' subtle non-verbal cues – line of sight, voice direction and body posture – in order to learn what a new word refers to.

At about eighteen months, babies are still speaking in one-word sentences, but a new insight into the nature of words means that they no longer use each word in one particular context only. The new words that they learn will now often refer not just to particular objects or events, but to categories of objects or events. Sometimes

Opposite: 'See!' serves as a one-word sentence to draw everyone's attention to the bonfire. It will be some time before this child can string words together, but already he can communicate efficiently.

the baby may over-extend the use of words. She may, for example, use the word 'dog' to refer not just to dogs but also to horses and cows. The word 'ball' may be used not only for balls but also for clocks and the full moon. At about this time, or sometimes slightly earlier, such over-extensions (calling all animals 'dog') become more common than under-extensions (using the word 'dog' only for their own dog, as if it were a proper name). Here are several typical examples of over-extensions from the developmental diaries:

> **Leslie (fifteen months):** We went to the zoo and just everything was 'ock' (dog). I kept saying 'monkey', 'elephant' etc. and she responded triumphantly 'ock'! She was very excited.

> **Nicky (sixteen months):** All birds are ducks to Nicky.

> **Sorsha (seventeen months):** We got a pumpkin today for Hallowe'en – Sorsha called it a 'ball' at first, and then we told her what it was and she said 'punky'.

> **Rowan (21 months):** The 'apple' for all fruit is wearing off as she knows they're not all the same and 'apple' is wrong but she doesn't know the right word.

The baby's tendency to use words to refer to categories of objects has been shown in recent experiments. Babies first see a small toy, such as a rabbit. Then they are given two more toys, one from the same category (another rabbit) and one that is related to the first toy in some other way (such as a carrot, which rabbits like to eat). In the experiments, the babies are divided into two groups. When the first object is shown to the first group, the experimenter just says: 'See this one', without giving a name to the object. This group is then told: 'Find another one', and has to choose between another object of the same category or another object related in a different way (like the carrot in the above example). By contrast, when the first object is shown to the second group, the experimenter says: 'See this dax.' In other words, this time the experimenter refers to the object with a word, òne that the baby doesn't already know. The second group is then told: 'Find another dax.' Babies in the group that hears the new word – 'another dax' rather than just 'another one' – are more likely to choose the object from the same category as the first 'dax'. Those in the group who only heard 'See this one' picked the other object. This finding suggests that babies of this age expect that first and foremost new words refer to object categories. This important understanding will be vital to babies' subsequent word learning, because nouns in the adult language refer to categories of objects.

Although babies may be limited to only single-word speech during this period, their language skills have progressed to the point where they can use them to communicate many different meanings. Words are now used for much more than directing other people's attention. They can serve to comment on a situation, person or object and they can be used to answer and ask questions. With real resourcefulness, the baby can use her body and intonation to make single words mean entire sentences! The same word can thus be a statement, a question or a demand. 'Dada!' said triumphantly as father enters the room is a statement, but 'Dada' said with rising intonation as the baby hears a car approaching is a question. Finally, 'Dada' said as the baby wants father to lift her from her high chair can be interpreted as a demand! The resourceful baby can now do a lot with single words. The parental reports illustrate this period of development:

> **Evelyn (thirteen months)**: Evy really can make herself understood these days with a combination of grunts, real words, and lots of gesturing about with her arms.

> **Neil (fifteen and a half months)**: He won't let up until he gets what he wants. He'll say 'bibi' which is his bottle with juice in it and he'll repeat 'bibi' loudly, making his intonation sound like an order. If he can't find it, 'bibi' is quieter, a bit like a query.

> **Ruth (sixteen months)**: I don't know how, but I seem to understand Ruth more this past week although she still isn't saying that much.

PUTTING WORDS TOGETHER

As mentioned earlier, babies' acquisition of new words is painstakingly slow during the first few months of their talking life. But around eighteen months of age, their vocabularies suddenly expand at a greatly increased rate. This period of rapid word learning has come to be known as the 'naming explosion'. From roughly eighteen months to six years of age, the baby will learn between six and ten new words per day! After the age of six, word learning levels off, and new words are again acquired at a slow rate. The diaries illustrate this progression:

Ruth (eighteen months): She's constantly asking 'what that?'.

Trevor (23 months): I'm amazed at how many words he remembers – he's always pestering me about the names of things. I don't know how he remembers them all because sometimes they only crop up a couple of times.

It is not clear what underlies babies' sudden and rapid rise in the rate of word acquisition. It may be due to changes in the brain, or it may simply be the result of the way in which all learning takes place: slow at first, with sudden increase, followed by a plateau. According to some researchers, the naming explosion marks the point in development at which babies attain 'nominal insight' – the knowledge that words stand for things and categories of things. But whatever its underlying cause, the naming explosion appears to be a universal phenomenon, occurring in babies learning languages around the world. Here are some examples of babies who appear to have entered the naming explosion:

Danielle (eighteen months): We were locked out of the house the other day so we sat in the car and I was naming different parts of the car, like the wheel, handbrake, gear, etc. I named about ten objects only once and I asked her where they were and she pointed to practically all of them and tried to say some of them.

Sorsha (eighteen months): Sorsha is just parroting every word she hears. Bren said 'That's crap' and she said 'crap'. We will have to watch our language now!

Kaspar (25 months): Kaspar never stops talking and is steadily increasing his vocabulary. He repeats everything he hears, for example the expression 'I know' even though he doesn't normally speak English and kept saying it. He evidently thought it meant he was saying 'No' to something. He repeats swearwords we came out with at an unguarded moment, and he keeps on saying Sheffield Wednesday (obviously without knowing what it means).

There's an important fact about the naming explosion. It always seems to coincide with the baby's first attempts to put words together. It seems that a critical amount of vocabulary is needed before the baby can begin to combine words into sentences. These first word combinations are not simply random – they are clearly rule-based, as the following examples show:

Tanya (seventeen months): She is starting to make up basic sentences, e.g. (Q) 'Is Tanya a baby?' (A) 'No, Tanya big girl'.

(**Two weeks later**): She is developing well in stringing words together – e.g., 'more dancing'.

Joshua (nineteen months): His language is beginning to sound more like proper English but he still doesn't say 'I' – instead he says 'Jos do it', 'Jos pain'. He's using strings of words together, not just one word. Yesterday he said 'naughty car, broken'.

Stacey (twenty months): Since we arrived in London Stacey's language has improved a lot. Here's my list of some of the things she's said this week:

> doggy gone
> big car
> my book
> Mummy book
> where Daddy
> good girl
> no bath

In most cases, toddlers combine an 'action' word with an 'object' word ('put sock'), but rarely two 'action' words ('put bring'). Often, one word will be used as a kind of 'pivot', around which other words may be attached. 'All-gone' ('All-gone baby', 'All-gone dog', 'All-gone bath') and 'more' ('more juice', 'more teddy') are commonly-used 'pivot' words of babies learning English. As these examples from the diaries illustrate, 'pivot' words may sometimes appear even before the second birthday:

Rowan (20 months): Commands: 'shoe me!', 'sock me!', 'juice me!', 'apple me!'.

Stacey (22 months): Today she started a new way of saying things – one word in front of everything: 'where Daddy/where bath/where baby'.

Jimmy (23 months): He certainly knows his own mind! He runs the words 'not go in' into one sort of word of his own: 'nogoin', and says that before everything he doesn't want, like 'nogoin juice', 'nogoin bath', 'nogoin nitenite' (to bed)!

One current topic of debate among researchers concerns the nature of the rules underlying the child's earliest word combinations. Some argue that these first rudimentary sentences are based on a set of rules that are unique to child language, that children have invented for themselves. Others point out that these first sentences may actually be based on the rules of adult grammar – but that because of limitations on how many words the baby can actually say at one time, they merely look 'childish'.

The debate is really about whether language is in-built, or whether it has to be entirely learnt during the first years of life. No one denies that experience – hearing a particular language and learning about the world – is crucial to the child's success at learning. After all, it is obvious that children in France tend to speak French, whereas children in Sweden usually speak Swedish. Clearly, input from the environment is important. At issue is how the baby *uses* her particular experience to come up with the grammar of her own language. For researchers who favour an explanation in terms of built-in properties, experience merely serves as a 'trigger' to lead children to acquire the grammatical system of their language. These researchers argue that the child comes equipped with a 'universal grammar' – basically a sort of a blueprint that can serve in the learning of any natural language. For other scholars, the environmental input plays a much more specific and fundamental role in the acquisition of grammar; according to them, children's knowledge of linguistic structure is largely built up by using their general intelligence to analyse the language they hear.

A major difficulty facing those who deny the existence of any innate blueprint for grammar is to account for how, during these first few years of life, babies develop such an intricate and elaborate system of linguistic rules. Bear in mind also that however rich the environmental input may be, it does not contain 'negative evidence' – information about what is not a grammatical sentence in the language. There are many examples of linguistic rules that young children seem to know but which they could probably never have 'learnt' from the environment. For example, babies of two years of age learning English will, in their spontaneous speech, say things like 'big girl', but they never seem to say things like 'big she'. Yet it isn't meaning that stops them doing so. After all, a girl can be referred to as either 'girl' or 'she'. So why not 'big she'? How did children learn these rules about permissible word combinations in English? Children of this young age apparently simply know that words belonging to some categories (nouns, like 'girl') can be preceded by adjectives (like 'big'), but that words belonging to other categories (pronouns, like 'she') cannot. No one ever teaches the child that she can't say 'big she' in English. Those who deny the child any prior linguistic knowledge have a hard time explaining how children might 'learn' rules such as these, and so early in life.

At this point in development babies take great pleasure in using speech to interact with others – so much so that they will actually say anything they can, even things that are patently untrue, just to sustain the conversation. Here are a couple of examples from the developmental literature:

Father: And he's kicking the ball. It's a big red ball.
Siobhan (two and a half years): I got a big red ball.
Father: No. Your ball's not red. Do you know what colour your ball is?
Siobhan: Brown ball.

Nathalie (six years): So tomorrow I'm going to school and we're going to do some special writing.
Simon (two years): I doing special writing.
Nathalie: Simon, that's not true. Daddy, Simon's telling lies again.
Simon: Telling lies again.
Nathalie: He's such a pain.
Simon: Such a pain.
Nathalie: Shut up, Simon, or I'll clonk you on the head.
Daddy: Leave him alone, Nathalie!

A parent will usually correct these untruths. However, one of the most striking findings in the study of child language is that although parents will correct children's language if it is untrue, they will rarely correct it if it is ungrammatical. So a child who says 'Boats go in the sky' might be corrected because she has made an error in meaning. But a child who says 'Boats goes in the water' might not be corrected, because she has 'only' made an error in grammar – she should have used the plural ('go'). A great deal of research has shown that parents tend not to provide children with so-called 'negative evidence' about grammar. If babies are never told which sentences violate the rules of their language, then they must be equipped with the impressive ability to learn language solely on the basis of 'good' sentences. Imagine trying to learn something by trial and error, but without ever knowing when you've made an error!

Also at this stage of language learning, babies often mimic everything that they hear without understanding much of what it means. This phenomenon is known technically as 'echolalia'. Children don't do this parroting with the intention of learning new sentences. Instead, their aim seems to be to get examples of language into their heads so that they can analyse its structure and form. Like an adult talking to himself to sort out something bothersome, the toddler parrots as one way of learning the complex rules of language and grammar. Here are two amusing examples from the diaries:

Rowan (21 months): Lots of echolalia – parroting meaningless words which are generally supplied by her sister (aged four), for instance, 'nightie night poo poo' always gets a laugh.

Alexandra (23 months): She listens to other people's conversations and repeats them. We were in Harrod's, and a lady was in the Cartier department saying, 'I want this one.' Her male companion said, 'That's all I hear: I want, I want, I want'. Then this little voice piped up, 'I want, I want, I want!' which had everyone laughing. When the radio is on she starts to sing a phrase that's just been on the radio. For example, if she hears Tina Turner singing 'Disco Inferno', she sings, 'Burn baby burn!' Or if it's 'Grease', she'll sing, 'You're the one that I want – ooh, ooh, ooh!'

BECOMING A COMPETENT TALKER

Finally, toddlers start to sound a bit more like adults. They talk in sentences of three or more words. And although their constructions are more complex than those of younger children, they still often fail to use little words like 'is', 'in', 'the', and 'do'. These are words that usually occur in non-stressed positions in sentences, and we saw earlier that babies tend to focus on stressed syllables when first learning language. Children will grapple with how to use these small words right up until about their third birthday. Some entries in the developmental diaries illustrate this stage of development:

Max (25 months): Max still doesn't use all the little words in sentences. He would say 'Max singing' instead of 'Max is singing'. He hasn't learnt about tenses so he will always say 'Max do it', not 'Max did it'.

Collin (27 months): He has been trying two or three word sentences, i.e. 'Hurt head'; Itchy leg'; 'mummy read book'; 'Daddy goes work'.

(One month later): Has added 'ing' to his words: 'I am standing'.Sometimes makes mistakes like 'I am sit up'. Using 'a' and 'the' more to connect words into a more correct sentence.

At two, when asked what's in his basket, the toddler will not only show the contents but will label them linguistically.

Gillian (23 months): She still leaves some words out, like the articles and sometimes the apostrophe 's', but we have no trouble understanding what she's trying to say: 'Mummy ring broken', 'Gilly knee hurt', 'Gilly got car', 'No in bath'.

Children generally understand many more words than they can say – and 'little words' like the articles 'the' and 'a' are no exception. Research has shown that seventeen-month-old babies who are at best using only single words, do none the less pay attention to whether there is an article in front of a word or not. Babies are shown two dolls and, pointing to one of the dolls, the experimenter says: 'That's Gorp'. The toddler is then asked: 'Show me Gorp.' In other parts of the experiment, the experimenter says: 'That's a gorp.' Toddlers are then asked: 'Show me a gorp.' In the first case, they point only to the same doll as the one the experimenter pointed to, but in the second case, where an indefinite article is used, they point to either one of the two dolls. This finding suggests that well before the age at which toddlers put articles into their own speech, they understand that no article implies a proper name ('Gorp') and the presence of an article implies a common noun ('a gorp').

Why do young children leave out the little 'function' words (like 'the' or 'and') when they first begin to combine words? One possibility is that parents rarely use these words and therefore children don't know that they are part of the language. In fact, this is not so. Function words are among the most frequent that parents use and that children hear. But although toddlers leave function words out of their own speech initially, experiments have shown that they know something about the need for functions words. Two-year-old children heard various simple, short sentences instructing them to do something. Sometimes the sentences were normal adult-like English including function words – a sentence like 'Give me the ball'. But other times the sentences omitted the function words; children simply heard: 'Give ball' – in other words, 'sentences' similar to the language they themselves produced. Which of these two sentence types would the toddlers be more likely to understand? The results were striking: two-year-olds performed better in response to the adult-like sentences. So although children of this age leave out the function words in their own speech, they seem to be sensitive to their presence in adult speech and understand sentences better when they are more adult-like. Why do toddlers leave out function words? First, function words are usually not stressed. We've seen evidence of toddlers' preference for stressed syllables over non-stressed ones when learning new words like giraffe (raffe). Second, there's a limit at this age on how much children are capable of saying, and function words carry less meaning than nouns and verbs.

The short sentences that older toddlers produce are similar to the language used to write telegrams – they are grammatical but concise, and they obey the word order of their native tongue. More than anything else, toddlers' mistakes reveal their amazing grasp of the rules of grammar. Because they have learnt them so well, they tend to overapply them. At this stage toddlers may add 's' to form all plurals, saying not only 'dogs' and 'chairs', but also 'tooths', 'foots' and 'mans'. They may add 'ed' to form all past tenses, using correct words like 'walked' and 'shouted', but also saying 'wented', 'bringed' and 'eated'. And they may add 'est' to form all superlatives, extending the correct forms like 'fastest' and 'slowest', to words like 'goodest' and 'worstest'. Here are some amusing examples:

Gillian (34 months): Gillian's now making quite a lot of errors. Today she was quite het up with Jeremy and I heard her say 'I goed to school, not Jemy'!

Janet (37 months): We took her to St James Park near the ponds and we saw some geese which she called 'gooses'! This is typical right now, e.g. she also says 'sheeps' when we look at the farm book.

By this point, children start to pronounce language the way adults do. Certain sounds may have yet to be mastered, particularly those that are more difficult for the articulatory apparatus of the mouth – for example, sounds associated with the letters 's', 'z', 'th', 'r', and 'f'. The more complex sounds made by clusters of consonants like 'st' and 'sp' also develop later, so words like 'sticky' or 'spade' may still come out as 'ticky' or 'tade'. Here are two examples:

Natasha (31 months): Enjoys saying 'double decker bus' constantly but has trouble with it – likewise with 'double buggy' which she shares with Xavier.

Janet (36 months): There's one word Janet still can't get her tongue around: 'shovel' which she says as 'sobel'.

Finally, one of the best strategies for learning more language also develops around this time. Toddlers ask questions. By asking 'what?', 'where?', 'why?' and 'who?', they can learn new names and discover still more about the rules of speech.

Kate (25 months): Kate is into the 'why' stage – she can be quite annoying. Everything I tell her to do, she responds 'why'. I don't think she's really asking a question, it's more automatic than that.

Stacey (26 months): For the past week she's been constantly asking questions: 'where Daddy?', 'where going?', 'What dat?'

Janet (35 months): Janet has started asking questions about language. Like she'll ask what something is called and then she'll ask why it's called that.

Toddlers will learn more than 60 new words each week over the next four years or so. Now language becomes a means for learning more about the world, as the diaries show:

Kaspar (26 months): Kaspar is trying to come to terms with the concept of time passing. He doesn't understand 'later' or 'tomorrow' but knows what 'waiting' means (that some things don't happen immediately). He is very eager to learn about everything around him (how traffic lights work, the difference between big and small, etc.).

Far right: by the age of three, children have grasped the rules of grammar and have a large vocabulary. Now they can start to have real conversations about the past, present and future, and about both real and imaginary worlds.

The two-year-old-child has already mastered much of the basic structure of her native language. At about this age she begins to develop a new kind of sensitivity to language – what is called 'meta-linguistic' awareness. For the first time, she starts not only to understand and produce speech herself, but also to think about the way language works. It is as if language has now become an object to explore in its own right, rather than just a means of communication. First, children begin to make spontaneous corrections to their own speech – to the choice of a word, its pronunciation, or to the order of words in a sentence. In addition, children start to ask questions about the appropriate word to use or about how to pronounce it. Typically they might ask: 'Is it "adult" or "a dult"'? Children also begin to comment on others' speech – correcting, say, a younger sibling's pronunciation. And they show the first signs of an ability to play with language – to use rhymes and to make puns. At this age, too, they start to be able to make judgements about language – to be able to decide whether an utterance is grammatical or ungrammatical. In one experiment, two-year-olds were asked to judge whether sentences were 'silly' or 'good'. They then heard sentences which were either perfectly grammatical (like 'Bring me the ball') or ungrammatical in some way (like 'Ball me the bring'). Although children this young were not very good at this task, their performance nonetheless suggested that they had some early sensitivity to the structure of language. By the time they are four, they can do these tasks easily. At that age, too, they are able to make

judgements about whether a sentence is polite or impolite. In another experiment, four-year-olds were asked to decide which of two speakers would be more successful in getting what he wanted from an old woman puppet, one who made a polite request (like 'I would like a sweet') or one who said something more direct (like 'I want a sweet'). Children of this age knew they would be more likely to get sweets if they used the polite form. A final indicator of children's early meta-linguistic awareness can be seen in their questions about other languages.

A number of different skills underlie the behaviours we have just noted. Among these skills is children's ability to monitor what they are saying – to listen to themselves as they speak. Another skill is the ability to check the result of what they have said – after they have spoken, to note if they have been fully understood. Additional metalinguistic skills appear in slightly older children, particularly the ability to appreciate rhymes, puns and riddles. These and other abilities characterise the meta-linguistic knowledge of older children and adults. It is striking that they first begin to appear in children as young as two or three years of age:

> **Gillian (35 months):** Gilly keeps correcting everything. She hates it if we imitate her way of pronouncing words. If I read her a story and I even slightly change the words, she screams, No! I have to get the words just right.

> **Janet (37 months):** Janet corrects her baby brother now – if he says 'bockle', she shouts, 'No, boTTle!'

By around three years of age, their knowledge of the world is expanding and their grasp of language is so sophisticated that children no longer speak only about the here and now. They tell their parents about the experiences they've had away from home and express feelings and beliefs, as the diaries illustrate:

> **Colin (28 months):** He now tells long stories about his day, a book he has had read to him, or repeating a conversation.

With fewer than 1,000 days of exposure to language, the toddler can talk about the past, the present and the future, can often use some specialist vocabulary and knows hundreds of different words. Of course, she still has to learn other things about language during the next few years, but already by this age she has mastered the most fundamental elements of her native tongue. She has become – to anyone who hears her – a competent member of the speaking world.

CHAPTER FIVE

THE WORLD OF THINKING

'But why can't I walk on water?', 'Why does the sun go to sleep at night?', 'Why does ice cream melt if I hold it in my hand?' These typical questions from three-year-olds capture a special feature of human intelligence: we don't just notice what happens in the world, we constantly strive to explain why things happen. And one of the ways in which babies discover how and why the physical world functions the way it does is by playing.

To any onlooker, babies' play may appear to be simply a way of passing the time. But play serves a far more important function: it leads babies to explore the similarities and differences amongst the things that they encounter in the world – bouncy rubber balls, fluffy teddies, rigid building blocks and flying aeroplanes, as well as meowing cats, leaping frogs, scurrying squirrels and flying birds. It is through play that the baby learns the necessary behaviours for becoming an effective explorer, scientist and inventor. In fact, what we may consider a mindless pastime is actually hard work for the baby! Simply by playing, she embarks on the long road to becoming a competent thinker. One parent already sees his child as a serious thinker:

> **Benji (seven weeks):** Benji is a very serious child. He can spend
> hours watching his mobile turn. His face is very serious, like a
> wrinkled old man thinking. We tend to disagree on whether he
> really can think – but he spends ages studying things already.

In the areas of development that we've examined so far – learning to walk, to use tools, to talk – many signs of the drive to learn have been obvious in the baby's actual behaviour. But thinking goes on inside the head, and newborn babies show relatively few outward signs of seeking to understand events in the physical world. There are not many entries in the developmental diaries about this early period,

Crying is one of the baby's tools for making things happen. It allows her to predict future actions and may be one of the first signs of her understanding of the laws of cause and effect.

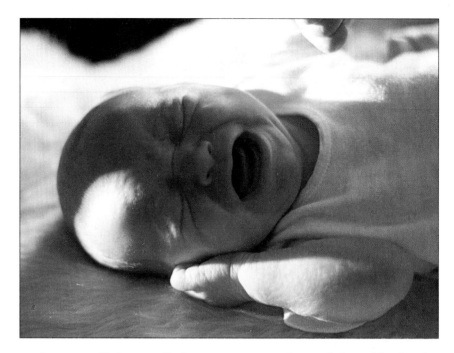

and so we will focus a little more on experimental data. Yet despite the fact that thoughts are not visible, researchers have uncovered many early signs of the baby's knowledge of the physical world. Early understanding is, of course, limited. But later, as babies learn to walk and talk, their constant struggle to make sense of the physical world becomes increasingly apparent.

THE CRYING GAME

It isn't obvious that crying has anything to do with becoming a scientist! Yet crying enables babies to discover some rudimentary examples of cause and effect. At roughly six to eight weeks of age, babies often pause between bouts of crying and quieten down for a moment as they try to attract attention. If they can't hear their parents' footsteps, they will cry a little more and pause again, until they have succeeded in getting what they want. Crying is one of babies' earliest ways of making things happen – it allows them to predict future actions. If crying isn't obviously a part of scientific practice, the prediction of events clearly is!

> **Laura (nine weeks):** As soon as I sit down to read, Laura starts to whine and then to cry fullblast. It's as if she knows I am busy with something else and uses her tears to get me to get up and come across to her. I've tried distracting her with toys, but she clearly wants me to interact with her 100% of the time.

Through routines which they both learn, parent and child jointly establish the meaning of different cries. These routines surround mundane daily activities like eating, sleeping and nappy-changing. And as each routine becomes more fixed in babies' memories, they cry in different ways to get the type of response they want. They begin to obtain some early answers – as well as some new questions – about how events happen in the world. Crying is the first outward sign that babies are gaining control and organising their world through intentional action, as the diaries illustrate:

> **Laura (nine weeks):** She's changed the way she cries over the last week or so. I can almost tell what she wants even before I get to her room, and I get the impression that she's listening out for my footsteps coming and that makes her stop crying even before I've actually got there to tend to her. What a little madam! She's got me twisted round her fingers already!

> **Lily (three and a half months):** Lily follows me with her eyes around the room and will cry if I walk away. As I write this she has started to cry purely to regain my attention.

> **Sarah (four months):** Sarah has definitely worked out how to get our attention. She cries louder and louder if we don't come straight away. It doesn't sound the same when she's wet and uncomfortable.

As the baby learns about how she can control her environment by crying, she inserts short pauses in her outburst to see if her crying has had its effect. **Over:** if the parent doesn't come during a pause the baby will cry even louder.

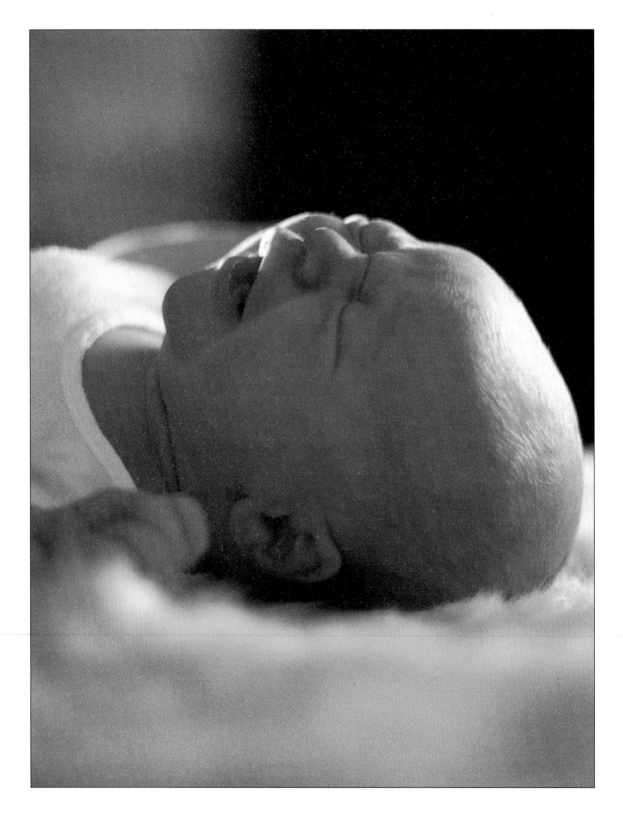

THE DEVELOPING BRAIN

As the baby interacts with the outside world during her first year of life, many fundamental changes take place in her developing brain. The baby's cortex will progressively take over from the subcortical reflexes, and simple voluntary acts will start to become possible. The subcortex will continue to play a role in behaviour, but with development different areas of the cortex and subcortex will become increasingly connected. These different circuits involve intention (motivational factors), motor control, attention, perception and memory. As a result of these increased connections, the brain will become more capable of complex and integrated acts such as those needed for attention, thinking, planning, and problem solving.

So babies soon gain voluntary control over their attention. A part of the brain deep in the inner folds of the cortex (the anterior cingulate gyrus) seems to be responsible for inhibiting the baby's automatic attention to things she sees, hears or touches. This part of the brain makes it possible for her to shift her attention in a voluntary way. A part of the cortex at the front of the brain (the dorsolateral prefrontal cortex) is the last to mature. Circuits in this part of the brain appear to be responsible for planning, delaying responses, and integrating different pieces of information that are separated in time and space – in other words, information that is absent at the current moment of planning. Indeed, cells in this part of the cortex have what are called 'memory fields': they are active only when information is being processed about objects that are not in view – information about where they were and when they were in that location (spatial and temporal information). Such details are obviously important for object permanence and planning. Experiments with monkeys have shown that if there is damage to this front part of the cortex, then the monkey can neither hold a goal in mind nor direct its attention in a voluntary way. Finally, another part of the brain (the hippocampus) becomes increasingly important for memory, particularly for children's explicit understanding of the world.

Just as thinking and language develop extensively over all the pre-school and early school years, so there are important reorganisations in the brain. It is thought that three waves of brain development characterise this period. Between one and a half to three years, the left hemisphere takes over major new functions; between four and five years, the right hemisphere develops many new connections; and between five and a half to six and a half years, it is again the turn of the left hemisphere to undergo further restructuring. After children learn to read, additional reorganisations occur in the back or posterior part of the brain.

In Chapter 1 we mentioned some of the early changes in the brain – that the cortex gradually becomes more dominant as a function of maturation and the baby's interaction with the environment. This two-way relationship between the brain and the child's expanding activities continues into middle childhood and beyond. And it is in later years that the human brain seems to differ most extensively from that of our closest relative in the animal world – the chimpanzee. At birth we share some 99 per cent of our genes with the chimpanzee. So there is very little difference between the genetic make-up of child and chimpanzee. But as children develop, it becomes clear that this small difference is a crucial one. Humans go on to become teachers, scientists, linguists, mathematicians, artists and technicians. Chimps, of course, do not. It is at around three years of age that the reorganisations of the human brain give rise to the creative thinking capacities that make children differ radically from chimpanzees. As one specialist in ape research, David Premack, put it: 'a good rule of thumb has proven to be: if the child of three-and-a-half years cannot do it, neither can the chimpanzee'. So later developments are essential to the child's becoming a little scientist of a uniquely human kind, however rich her initial knowledge may be.

REASONING ABOUT OBJECTS AND NUMBERS

Until recently, researchers had thought that young babies could conceive only of the 'here and now' – the visible or the touchable. According to this traditional view, 'out of sight' was, literally, 'out of mind'. But as we learnt in Chapter 3, the results of new studies suggest that even quite young babies do seem to know that objects that they can no longer see or touch continue to exist. Babies as young as three or four months of age show surprise when they see events that violate the idea that objects are permanent. They look astonished when a train engine seems to pass right through a toy blocking a railway track. Without an understanding of the permanence of objects – in particular, the fact that they are solid – babies would show no concern at all about such puzzling displays. Object permanence, then, is an essential piece of young babies' mental equipment, one that helps them to become effective thinkers.

Babies also appear to be mathematicians, and from early on they are sensitive to differences in small numbers like one, two and three.

Although this is not easy to see in babies' everyday behaviour, parents do sometimes note such abilities:

> **Sarah (five months):** Sometimes we play games after she's finished eating in the high chair. She loves one where I take a few of her toys, hide them under the table top shouting 'all gone' and then making them pop up again just after. She squeals with delight. I once dropped one of the three toys we were playing with by mistake, and I could swear she looked a bit puzzled when I put only two toys back on her table.

Experimental findings suggest that some basic understanding of number may be present at a very young age. Babies of three to four months were shown an image of three different toys which flashed up on a screen – say, a teddy, a ball, and a cube. The image then changed, and babies were next shown three new toys – say, a cup, a spoon and a bottle. The image kept changing, revealing each time a new set of three different toys. The babies' interest gradually waned, and they paid less and less attention to the image. They became bored. At one point, however, the image changed in a new way. Instead of showing a set of three toys, it now showed only two toys. The babies suddenly looked for much longer – they seemed to be reacting to something new. Recall that throughout the experiment they kept on seeing pictures of new toys. So what became boring could not have been the content of the pictures. Instead, it must have been the one thing common to all the displays: the fact that whatever the objects were, there were always three of them. A display with two objects was suddenly more interesting. The same occurred when a series of images of two objects was followed by an image of three. These findings suggest that at this very young age babies do have some appreciation of 'two-ness' versus 'three-ness'.

Another related experiment showed that babies' sense of numbers up to three may be quite sophisticated. In this new experiment, babies saw two screens. A picture of two objects appeared on one screen. On the other appeared a picture with three objects. A loudspeaker was placed between the two screens. When two drumbeats sounded from the loudspeaker, the babies tended to look at the screen that showed two objects. But when three drumbeats sounded from the loudspeaker, the babies then preferred to gaze at the screen with three objects. So babies' understanding of the numbers up to three is not only an appreciation of what these quantities look like. Babies are also able to match the sound of two or three with the sight of two or three – they appear to be able to 'cross-modal' match, an ability we saw in an earlier chapter. Although babies under six months of age can't distinguish numbers above three, they do have a clear sense that two is different from three.

Babies even appear to know how to do basic arithmetic. In recent studies, five-month-olds watched as a Mickey Mouse doll was placed on a table in front of them. A screen was then moved in front of Mickey Mouse, so that the babies could no longer see him. The babies then watched as a hand brought in a second Mickey Mouse, and placed him behind the screen as well. The screen was then removed. One group of babies saw two Mickey Mouses on the table – the expected outcome. Another group – through a clever trick – saw only one Mickey Mouse. Those who saw only one Mickey Mouse looked longer at the table – they seemed to be surprised when the screen was removed, as if their expectations had been violated. They somehow knew that one Mickey Mouse plus one Mickey Mouse ought to equal two Mickey Mouses. In other parts of the experiment, they expected that two Mickey Mouses plus one Mickey Mouse should equal three Mickey Mouses, and they showed surprise when it didn't. In other words, they seemed to be able to do very simple addition. The same surprise occurred when the experiment involved subtraction. So when three Mickey Mouses were first placed on the table, the screen brought in, and then one Mickey Mouse was visibly taken away, the babies seemed to expect to see two Mickey Mouses left. They showed surprise if there were still three when the screen was removed. In other words, they seemed to know something about very simple subtraction. This early facility with small quantities gives babies a way of keeping track of how many things they are dealing with at any given time, and of predicting how many objects should be there as a result of their own actions.

As they get older and become more competent speakers, toddlers start to learn the counting sequence, as the diaries illustrate:

Genevieve (nineteen months): This week I gave her a bottle of juice during a meal. When she finished I brought a second with milk. She put the two side by side and said 'two'. Other times she has simply repeated my last word but this time the 'two' was not a mimic of what I said!

Collin (27 months): He recognises numbers written from one to ten and can name them (he has learnt this from his *This Old Man, He Played One* book). He can name numbers out of sequence.

Another time he was playing with a complex activity cube puzzle at a friend's home. He found a slightly abstract figure four. He named it and patiently turned the cube to find the four-hole. He showed covert problem solving to insert the shape correctly. I was surprised to see this!

One can often hear parents on a staircase counting each of the stairs to their toddler as they go down them together: 'and one, and two, and three, and four, and five'. The diaries provide another example of such parental behaviour:

> **Nadiyah (ten months):** She points to her fingers (like she sticks her forefinger out and touches the tip with her other one). When she does this, I count 'one, two, three, four, five,' and she smiles. When Nadiyah does this and I see her do it – I always count for her.

Toddlers soon learn to imitate the counting sequence. But what do they make of this game? At first they are probably doing little more than reciting. But their earlier focus on quantity soon links up with the counting game. Experiments have shown that almost as soon as they start counting, young children adhere to a few basic how-to-count principles. Some toddlers follow the correct counting sequence; others might count: 'one, two, seven, four, nine'! The words they actually use don't matter. 'One, two, three' is what we say in English, but it's *un, deux, trois* in French, and *eins, zwei, drei* in German. As pointed out in Chapter 4, words have arbitrary relations with the things that they stand for, and numbers are no exception. What is important is that whatever the list that the child invents, the words always appear in the same order. After all, the words for our number sequence could have been: 'one, two, seven, four, nine' and actually have meant the first five numbers of the list.

To count successfully, toddlers must respect some implicit rules: don't count any one object twice (one-to-one correspondence principle); always say the numbers in the same order (stable-order principle); and, finally, let the last number reached stand for the total number of objects counted (cardinality principle). In addition, no particular object has to be, say, the 'one' or the 'six', so the toddler can count a group of, say, six objects starting and ending with a different object each time she counts them.

Experimental evidence suggests that toddlers may readily grasp the one-to-one and stable-order principles. They count each object only once, and they always count in the same order. But initially toddlers don't really understand the cardinality principle. If two- to three-year-olds are asked: 'How many toys are there?', they will often succeed in counting the six toys in a pile. However, if they are told: 'Give me three toys', most toddlers simply take a handful without counting. They don't realise how counting can be used when asked a different question. In other words, they don't really understand the cardinality principle implicit in their ability to count. What appears to be real counting is something toddlers can only do when they are specifically asked: 'How many?'. They still have to get a deeper knowledge of what it means when they recite the counting sequence. Only then can they successfully solve other tasks that involve a true understanding of numbers.

DIFFERENTIATING KINDS OF OBJECTS

As well as their interest in how many objects are present, babies also focus on similarities and differences between various kinds of objects. From early on, human babies have a drive to sort objects into basic categories. So babies play with a toy aeroplane in a different way from the way they do with a toy bird, suggesting that they somehow know that inanimate objects like aeroplanes move differently from animate objects like birds. They tend to push an aeroplane along a table or in the air in a smooth, straight line (mechanical motion), whereas they make the bird hop along the table and change direction several times (biological motion).

Researchers have come to similar conclusions about young babies' knowledge of the difference between mechanical and biological movement. Consider a dot that appears in the corner of a television screen. If the dot moves across the screen in a wiggly line, stopping from time to time, and then continuing, we would probably think it represented something animate. This is the way in which biological objects normally move. By contrast, if the dot moved on a straight path across the screen, hit the side and moved again on a straight path, we would probably take it to represent an inanimate object, because this is how mechanical objects usually move. Even three- and four-month-old babies appreciate the difference between these two types of movement. If they repeatedly watch a dot moving across a screen in an animate fashion, they get bored. However, when the dot suddenly starts to move in an inanimate fashion, their interest is renewed. The reverse is also true: babies show increased interest when an inanimate dot changes into an animate one. Recall that all along they've simply been watching a dot moving across on a screen. If they hadn't noticed the different types of movement, then they would have remained bored throughout, even when the type of movement changed. But they don't. They pay attention to differences in movement made by different objects. This helps them to categorise objects and not to confuse, for example, a real rabbit munching on a carrot in his cage with an identical-looking mechanical wind-up rabbit in the toy box!

Experiments conducted with babies of about ten months of age reveal still further their ability to differentiate between animate and inanimate objects. In one of these studies, babies were given a series of plastic toy aeroplanes one at a time – a glider, then a jumbo jet, then a fighter plane. As they saw aeroplane after aeroplane, the babies got bored; they started to play with each successive toy for a shorter period of time. But when the babies were then given a plastic toy bird with outstretched wings – an object that looked remarkably similar to the aeroplanes in both size and shape – their interest was suddenly renewed, and they played with the bird for a long time. It is as if the babies appreciated the essential difference between inanimate kinds of object (aeroplanes) and animate ones (birds), even when they look alike. So already during the first year of life, babies draw distinctions amongst objects, distinctions that will greatly help them to sort things into increasingly complex categories.

APPRECIATING CAUSE AND EFFECT

Young babies have a further ability that helps them make sense of the physical world: an understanding of cause and effect. Young babies know that inanimate objects can be carried off by animate ones (like a hand), but not by other inanimate ones. They also know that an animate object must make contact with another object if it is to succeed in getting hold of it. In one experiment, seven-month-olds were first shown a film depicting a hand picking up a toy and carrying it away. After repeatedly seeing this sequence, the babies got bored, and looked at it for shorter and shorter periods. Then the sequence was changed in one small way. Through trick photography, the hand no longer actually made contact with the toy – there was a gap between the hand and the toy as they moved off together. Babies were surprised to see this altered sequence and their interest was suddenly renewed. This finding suggests that babies of this age understand that a human hand must be in contact with a toy in order to pick it up and carry it away. But babies don't apply this rule indiscriminately. They apply it only to animate things like hands. So when another group of babies was shown a sequence with something inanimate (a block) seeming to make contact with the toy before both moved away together, they got bored irrespective of whether the block was in contact with the toy or not. They apparently understood that an inanimate object like a block simply cannot 'pick up and carry away' a toy – whether or not it makes contact with it. So both inanimate sequences were considered the same. By contrast, for the first group of babies the two sequences – one with the hand touching the object, the other with a gap between the hand and the object – had different meanings. They had clear expectations of what hands can and cannot do.

Babies' grasp of cause and effect is subtle in other ways, too. Consider what is known as the 'Michotte effect'. This simple phenomenon can be demonstrated by using two objects like billiard balls, one of which is made to collide with the second, which immediately moves off on its own. As adults, we view this event as an example of cause and effect: we see the first billiard ball (the cause) actually making the second billiard ball move (the effect). But what about infants? They, too, seem to interpret such events in a similar way to adults. In an experiment, one group of six-month-olds saw the following 'launching' sequence: an object (A) came in at the lefthand side of a screen, collided with another object (B) in the middle of the screen, and then B moved off to the righthand side. Babies repeatedly watched this event until they got bored. Then a change was introduced. This time there was a time delay between the moment when A made contact with B and the moment when B moved off to the right. In other words, A did not appear to cause B to move – it did not collide with B but simply came to rest momentarily next to it. Another group of babies first watched the normal launching sequence until they got bored, but this time the new event involved a spatial gap instead of a temporal gap between A and B. So although B took off as soon as A approached, A never actually touched B. In both groups, the babies seemed somewhat surprised when they saw the new sequence, as if they noticed the temporal delays and the spatial gaps.

Understanding cause and effect and predicting the outcome of events are essential to the child's growing knowledge about how the physical world functions. The diaries give a nice example of how babies predict events in a cause and effect sequence:

> **Theo (nine months):** Since Theo loves twiddling the dimmer
> switch on our lights, Eugene decided to give him a spare one he

had in his tool box. As Theo played with it, he kept looking up at the lights expecting them to dim.

As babies develop their understanding of cause and effect, they also become purposeful experimenters, as the parental diaries illustrate:

Taffy (ten and a half months): When splashing furiously in the bath she suddenly noticed the droplets running down the inside of the bath. This fascinated her and she watched intently until they disappeared and then she splashed again. This was repeated several times.

It is at this time, too, that babies carefully inspect the details of events and make predictions in advance of them actually happening, as the diaries illustrate:

Izzy (eleven months): He just figured out that he could see what was on the spoon before Mom put it in his mouth, thereby rejecting the courgette that snuck into the rice.

THE YOUNG EXPLORER AND IMITATOR

Young babies have a sophisticated and detailed understanding of the physical world – an understanding that researchers have brought to light without even requiring the babies to leave their mother's laps! But of course babies don't just sit there watching the world go by. They are far from passive, and once they start to crawl and walk they move about unfamiliar settings with an insatiable curiosity. They behave like intrepid explorers, touching everything in sight as they try to work out how the objects in the room function. Their understanding may sometimes be incomplete – they may, for example, learn simply that a toy engine makes a loud noise when it's thrown to the floor. They may be taken aback when pushing a button makes a cassette jump out of its container. When babies explore in this way, they appear to have no specific motive other than simply to enjoy themselves. But this is work, not play. Their repeated actions show their determination to understand how things function. Babies are running little experiments, even if rather unsystematically. Exploration of this kind is vital to their learning such concepts as over and under, up and down, big and small, in and out. It helps babies to make sense of their world, a world whose contents do not always behave predictably! Here's a diary entry about a young explorer:

Exploring a complex new environment is work, not play: this baby is learning about the properties of different objects and what he can do with them.

Morgan (ten months): She opens and closes all types of doors/cupboards/lids with ease. She can also press buttons and flick switches. She also tries to open packets and screw lids but with no success, but I think she understands the concept.

Imitating what they've seen their parents do, babies try out the alluring buttons on the hi-fi and television. This activity helps them to learn that cause and effect isn't always straightforward. The baby may first react with surprise when she aims her index finger at a button and the music stops. But by doing so repeatedly, she soon masters the idea that certain buttons do things that other buttons don't. Only some buttons 'cause' the music to stop, even if it's not visibly apparent why they do. The following examples from the developmental diaries demonstrate this general phenomenon:

Marko (thirteen months): This last week Marko has decided to push every button in the house to see what it does. If it does something, he does it again and again. He especially likes the CD player 'ON' button because when he pushes it he gets a little light-show.

Nicky (fifteen and a half months): He loves electrical equipment and delights in turning the telly button on and off and of course destroying cassette tapes.

Babies soon begin to refine the concepts that they acquired earlier. Their explorations now start to become exceedingly thorough – sometimes too thorough for their parents' liking! Taking a cupboard

The toddler has developed a sophisticated understanding of the laws of cause and effect: he experiments with different buttons to see what happens.
Over: for these two children this playroom is like a scientist's laboratory where they can each discover things relevant to their level of development.

Imitating their immediate role models helps children to explore the social and physical world they inhabit.

apart satisfies an apparent urge to break up things into their basic parts. The baby is dissecting objects much as a biologist would dissect a frog. Puzzles are more interesting when taken apart than when put together. Containers of Lego are better emptied of their contents and turned upside down. Through their play, babies are now learning a new way to categorise objects – into the containers and the contained. This new discovery may not always lead to a positive outcome – the rubber ball in the bowl of porridge won't taste particularly good – but the baby has secured another foothold in understanding and manipulating the physical world. Here's a typical example from the diaries:

> **Danielle (sixteen months):** She opens my kitchen cupboards, takes out all my tins, puts them by the sink, and when she's had enough she puts them back again. She also likes taking things out of her toy box and putting them back.

Another way in which babies learn about the world of objects is by imitating their immediate role models, their parents. They want to copy everything adults do, even if they don't understand the principles involved. They may easily run into trouble: helping father with vacuuming the carpet can lead to the disappearance of a favourite small toy; and cleaning the bath with mother's silk scarf can ruin it! But imitation is a powerful learning tool for babies. And they can copy what they've seen others do, even if they can't yet innovate.

Later developments will enable the baby to combine objects and their functions in novel, imaginary ways:

Theo (ten months): He copied me brushing my hair the other day, and now he brushes his hair with everything brush-like, including the broom and the nailbrush. When he saw me shaving my legs this morning, he tried to help using the spoon he was holding!

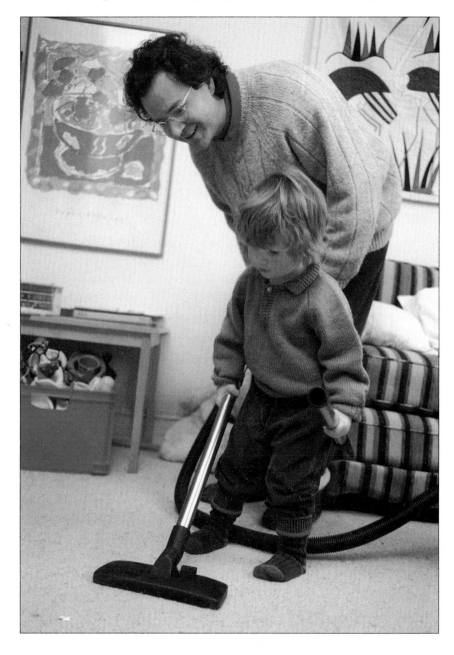

This young boy is imitating what he sees his father do as he cleans the house, and learning to operate machines he will find important later on.

185

So imitation is a vital stepping-stone on the path to human creativity. But for the time being, it simply provides some of the ingredients of later pretend play. The diary examples below indicate how babies use imitation to gain an understanding of how objects work. Of course, much has yet to be learnt. Sleeping with a toy vacuum cleaner or washing the floor with a clean tea-towel are hardly appropriate acts! But through their imitation babies are on the path to successfully learning about objects:

> **Nicky (fifteen and a half months):** Nicky absolutely adores the Hoover. It's his obsession, along with dustpans, brushes, mops, etc. He pulls them out of the cupboard and cleans the house whenever he can. I bought him a mini-Hoover and the first night he had it, he insisted on taking it to bed with him!

> **Danielle (sixteen months):** This morning I was washing up and when I looked around, she had the tea towel on the floor and was cleaning the floor as she saw me do yesterday.

THE PROBLEM-SOLVER

Babies will gain further insight into the workings of objects by learning how to solve problems. At about six months, they are capable of sophisticated voluntary actions. Getting at a favourite toy that is out of reach requires careful forethought. The baby needs to work out what the toy is standing on and whether it can be pulled

This baby has hardly learned to sit and she is already solving complex problems. She sees a desired object outside the playpen ...

Concentrating hard, she pulls the toy to the edge of the playpen …

She solves the problem of how to get the toy through the bars by turning it on one side and twisting it. This is not aimless play but careful planning.

187

towards her. And once a toy is brought close to the playpen bars, the baby has to work out how to get it inside. A toy rabbit may be simply too big to pull straight through! Babies can often be seen frowning as they assess a problem and work out a solution. Their success at dealing with situations like this is an indication of their newly-acquired capacity for recalling the results of trial and error and carrying out simple problem-solving. In Chapter 3, we described an experiment that demonstrated babies' increasing adeptness at problem-solving over the course of the first year. Older babies were more likely than younger ones to pull on the corner of a cloth to obtain a desirable toy which had been placed on top of the cloth but out of reach. Actions of this sort are not species-specific, since chimpanzees in the wild are capable of similar feats. But they are still impressive, and they will become even more so as the baby quickly progresses beyond these relatively simple tasks.

A few months into their second year, toddlers grow more 'scientific' and start to understand that the physical world follows certain laws. Even early on babies realise that objects dropped from their hands will fall downwards, and that one solid object can't pass through another one. Where babies differ from older children and adults is in understanding how to apply these laws and how to make exceptions.

Bathtime is a privileged moment for exploration and discovery. Babies have yet to learn how water is different from air, and how this difference affects the way objects behave. An air-filled plastic duck resists the baby's attempts to push it down in the water. Yet the baby may doggedly persist in trying to keep the duck under water and to make it obey the laws of gravity that she thought applied to everything. It is by being more experimental that the baby learns about the different properties of water. She may vary the depth from which she releases the duck to watch it shoot out of the water to different heights. She may then feel the water resist her hand differently as she pushes the duck deeper and deeper. And she brings another surprisingly valuable quality to this novel learning experience: an unwillingness to relinquish her beliefs about the world in the face of a few counter-examples. She keeps trying out a new idea, even when it doesn't work. Without this useful piece of mental equipment, babies would be stymied in their ability to hold on to hypotheses and build mini-theories about the world. At this age, when their ideas about the laws of physics are violated, they tend to ignore the counter-examples. Like some scientists, babies look to the world to confirm their theories about it – not to falsify them!

Far left: toddlers have a passion for sorting objects. They will spend hours putting them in and out of containers, and dividing them by colour, shape and size.

189

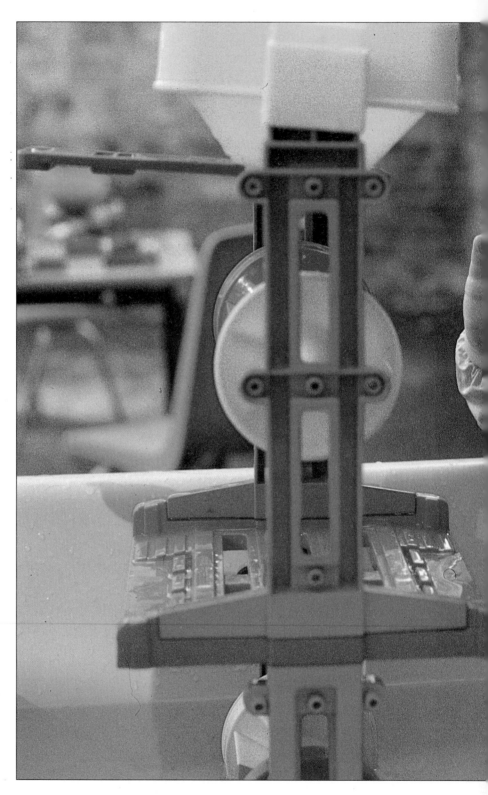

Through the hard work
of play this youngster
will learn about the
different properties of
liquids and solids, and
what happens when you
mix them: a small
scientist at work.

Only a few months later, the baby is able to put together her skills and knowledge in solving quite complex tasks. She is capable of coming up with solutions to problems such as how to reach a packet of biscuits that is on a kitchen shelf five feet from the ground. To solve this problem, she first needs to remember that her mother put the packet on the shelf several hours earlier. She must then plan her action by adapting the memory of her past experiences of climbing. She scans the room to see what could serve as a stool. She may see an empty plastic toy-box. But she will have to remember to turn it upside down to stand on it, or it won't make her taller. These and other ideas must be coordinated into a proper sequence, and then carried out. In the previous chapter, we saw that the ability to say single-word sentences is finally replaced by the capacity to form complex multi-word sentences. So, too, the ability to execute one-step plans is superseded by the capacity to string together a whole sequence of complicated thoughts and actions. Here is an example from the diaries:

> **Danielle (sixteen months):** She likes to try and work things out. She has a baby walker and couldn't get it into the kitchen because we have a gate across it and there is a little step. Eventually she worked out how to get it over the step and into the kitchen.

SORTING THINGS OUT

Babies show a constant drive to categorise what they observe in the world – the substances (water, sand, milk, jelly, toothpaste) and the objects (dogs, bananas, chairs, sticks, shoes). Close to their first birthday, they begin to learn about different kinds of material substances. They now pour water and sand into containers, and they start to realise that unlike water, sand can be built into castles. They also learn that sand mixed with water does something entirely different, squelching messily through their fingers. This sort of exploration is typical at this age:

> **Taffy (ten months):** Loves squishing jelly through the palm of her hand and watches it oozing through her fingers.

Babies thus come to learn the various ways in which substances can be distinguished and classified. Here's a good example from the diaries of a child who still has much to learn about the critical properties of both sand (not for eating!) and water (can surround people!):

Far left: even something as simple as opening a packet of sweets initially involves planning and problem solving, and requires the toddler's full concentration.

Theo (ten months): The first day we went to the beach, Theo crawled around on the sand and ate quite a lot of it. When he saw me get into the sea, he crawled towards me rapidly and looked very astonished when the water came up around him.

(**The same week**): Theo just loves swimming in the sea and in the swimming pool. He often puts his face down into the water to taste it. He does the same on the sands, tasting mouthfuls, and then looking rather surprised.

The diaries also provide an early example of how language and sorting interact:

Sorsha (seventeen months): Sorsha is starting to distinguish between certain similar things, for example, she now calls milk 'muck' and water 'woo-woo' instead of calling all drinks 'woo-woo'.

In addition to learning about substances, babies also start to grasp more about the different properties of objects. We've already seen how babies under twelve months old have worked out important differences amongst distinct types of objects – such as inanimates and animates. By half-way through their second year, toddlers have learnt much more about how to categorise objects. Having reached the 'naming explosion' described in Chapter 4, they now have a new ability with object classification – words. Not only do they constantly ask what things are called, they also begin to invent and refine categories of their own, deciding how they want to structure the world, rather than simply settling for how the world may happen to be presented to them. Babies become little 'sorters', and will spend hours of playtime separating objects into different categories. One day they may sort objects in one way; another day they may sort the same objects following a different idea. For example, if the baby stumbles upon a fruit bowl in the kitchen, she may first sort the pieces by colour – putting the yellow grapefruit and the yellow bananas together in one pile, and the red apple and red plums in another. Minutes later, she may sort the pieces again, but this time by shape – now placing the round grapefruit, apple and plums in one pile and the crescent-shaped bananas in another. Sorting objects by shape or by function is a particularly common phenomenon at this age, as the developmental diaries reveal:

Rowan (21 months): She is getting very good at sorting: will empty out the dishwasher of cutlery for me and put it in the right section – knife, spoon, fork. Loves doing it, too – very helpful.

(**Two months later**): Can spend an hour sorting money, cutlery or things into piles or jars, etc.

Max (23 and a half months): Max has started comparing objects. If he sees a penguin on the TV then he goes to his box of animals and picks out a penguin. He'll do the same with pictures. He also moves objects around and will line all his animals up on the settee and then move them all somewhere else.

Dominic (24 months): Sorts out bricks by colour and size and enjoys building with bricks.

Kaspar (26 months): Kaspar can sort things easily and put objects into groups. (He understands, for example, what animals belong in the zoo and what in the city farm.)

BEYOND THE HERE AND NOW

At about eighteen months, babies begin to engage in pretend play. This development gives them a final important tool for thinking flexibly about the world of physical objects. Consider this common scenario: a toddler arranges a tea set on a kitchen table with her older brother. She pours imaginary tea for her brother, who plays along in the game. If the brother takes his cup and upturns it, the toddler now pretends to wipe up the spillage from the floor! This type of pretend play is commonplace amongst children of this age. Even if it imitates exactly what happens in the "real" adult world, it is none the less highly complex. Children are able to sustain the pretence in all its detail. In addition to pouring the imaginary tea, they will put in two pretend lumps of sugar, carefully add non-existent milk, and offer it to a brother and a teddy bear to drink! They will pretend to check when the teapot is empty, and pretend to add more water. The sequence of actions is a highly accurate mimicking of real adult activities. But there is more to it than that. In such pretend play, the toddler treats the same teapot first as if it were full and then as if it were empty – even though it is really empty throughout. In pretend play like this children move beyond the here and now – from the real world to what is called the counterfactual world. They are no longer constrained by real events only, but can now entertain hypothetical ones. Here are some examples of this sort of play from the diaries:

Danielle (sixteen months): She gets her toy teapot and pours it into a cup and pretends to drink from it. She has a dolly that she

To sustain imaginary play the child goes beyond the here and now of the real world and into the counterfactual world: an empty teapot carefully fills an empty cup.

feeds a toy bottle to, and she has managed to get the teat of the bottle in the dolly's mouth.

Max (22 months): When the telephone rings, Max goes to pick up his pretend telephone and says hello. He will continue talking whilst you are on the phone, and then say good-bye when you do.

Only a year later, children display an ability for truly inventive play. Before this time, their pretend play was anchored in objects and events that were like those of the world of adults. But from about two and a half years, children begin to make up their own rules, and these are sometimes quite bizarre. 'Doctors' may offer treatment to non-existent patients. A Wendy house may become a castle. And the conversations in which children engage take them further into a complex fantasy world. Not only can objects become separated from their everyday functions, but also the child herself can become someone else, as the diaries show:

> **Ria (31 months):** Likes to pretend play. Wears my shoes and takes my bag to go shopping either to 'Sweetie shop' or 'Waitrose'. She is Mummy and everyone else is allocated a role. I am usually Ria or the ugly sister (reference to Cinderella)!

If imaginary water has been spilt, the child continues her counterfactual reasoning and wipes up the imaginary mess. Pretend play is in fact very intellectually demanding.

Two serious workers discovering the operation of a typewriter: the cause-effect relationship between pressing a key and making a mark on paper is being experimented with.

Imagination underpins scientific thought just as strongly as it does art. And so play of this sort is an important achievement in the baby's struggle to understand the material world. These examples from the diaries show highly complex and imaginative play:

Max (23 and a half months): Max does a lot of pretend play with his toys. He also improvises and uses objects and pretends they're something else, e.g. the remote control is sometimes a telephone and sometimes an electric shaver so he can shave at the same time as Mike.

Natasha (30 months): Natasha has started to pretend play on her own and acts out scenes from her video collection (*Peter Pan, Cinderella, Alice in Wonderland*) with her dollies all gathered around her. I overheard her telling them what she had done that day and what she was going to do: i.e. 'I've got a nice dress on', 'My house has just been painted' and 'I'm going to ride on a horse when my baby comes' are all sayings she repeats regularly.

At the same time as the young child is developing all her skills as a little scientist, her language is becoming increasingly sophisticated. It now shows signs that she is thinking about cause and effect and about how to explain what goes on in the world. Here's a typical conversation:

> **Ishbel (27 months)** is eating an ice cream with her mother and her younger brother, Duncan:
>
> **Mother:** How does it make you feel when you eat it?
>
> **Ishbel:** Cold!
>
> **Mother:** Do you think it makes him feel cold?
>
> **Ishbel:** It's cold because it's been in the freezer.
>
> **Mother:** Oh oh.
>
> **Ishbel:** He's ripped the tag.
>
> (Ishbel starts to talk about rabbits.)
>
> **Mother:** Is Duncan a rabbit?
>
> **Ishbel:** No, he's gonna be a tiger mask.
>
> **Mother:** So he's gonna wear a tiger mask, is he? I think I'd better clean him. Tell him to be careful.
>
> **Ishbel:** Be careful, Dunky. If you do that, you'll be crying and then

Even a plastic toy can start the child on the road to understanding the intricacies of something as complex as photography.

The simple game of playing at shopping requires many skills: remembering what one wants and what one has already taken; selecting the right quantity; knowing how much you can carry before you need a basket, and more. It is a serious learning process.

your mother has to put …er… up and don't ever do it again.
Mother: Did you get that, Duncan? Ishbel was telling you not to lean back in the high chair.

Despite the childlike nature of Ishbel's language, her sentence structures include words used for explanation – like 'because' – and those expressing hypothetical situations and cause and effect – like 'if...then'. By this age, children start to use complex language to express their knowledge about the relationships between events.

The child's long struggle to develop an adult-like understanding of the physical world continues well into middle childhood. Yet the very young infant is already equipped with a rich supply of resources for achieving this understanding. Important developments after infancy – as babies explore, imitate, solve problems, sort, and play – put them firmly on their path to becoming mature thinkers.

CHAPTER SIX

BORN TO BE SOCIAL

Babies are born into a social world. From birth, they find themselves surrounded by people who can sympathise with others, are aware of themselves, share emotional bonds, and – unlike any other species – know that other people have thoughts and memories different from their own. How does the baby acquire the mental skills that underly this social understanding?

The human baby seems to be a social being from the start. She spends much of her time watching other people, but she actually understands very little about them at first. She can't take their perspective, only her own. She doesn't even know that the baby she sees when she's in front of a mirror is, in fact, herself. She has only a very limited sense of herself as an individual, separate from but similar to the other people around her. She doesn't know that other people have minds and feelings of their own. Over the course of three short years, however, she will gradually master an impressive set of social skills.

A GROWING SENSE OF OTHERS

When they are just a few months old, babies already seem to be sensitive to other people's emotions. Not only does the baby smile when her mother smiles at her, but she reacts to her angry expression by looking angry and upset herself. But it would be premature to conclude from this behaviour that babies know how their mothers are feeling in such circumstances. It will be a long time before they can put themselves in other people's shoes. Instead, this early – and apparently social – behaviour is merely based on imitation. This is not to deny that such imitation is an important precursor to truly social understanding. For example, when the baby copies her mother's angry expression, the very movement of her own facial muscles may create a sensation of distress inside her. And so through

In the early months of life, the baby is fascinated by the world of people. This baby is smiling at his mother, but he would willingly smile at anyone who coos at him.

imitation, babies can start to develop associations between muscular reactions and emotional expressions.

During the first few months of life, the baby is fascinated by the world of people. But she is initially rather indiscriminate about whom she gives her favours to! She will smile and coo at almost anyone who smiles and plays with her. Her parents, of course, play a privileged part in her life, and the baby can recognise them as familiar faces or voices in the crowd. At this time, however, she treats her parents in much the same way as she does any other passer-by – that is, as someone to smile at.

But at about seven to nine months, things suddenly start to change. Not only has the baby learnt to recognise familiar people, she has also built up complex mental images of them. Several months of socialising have given her firm memories of people as individuals, not just as faces with happy or sad expressions. As a result of this mental development, the baby has become strongly attached to the one or two people who are constant in her life. Strangers who only weeks earlier would have been the objects of chuckles and happy gurgles, now become terrifying – so much so that the baby can't bear to be separated from her parent for even a few seconds. No one is sure why babies become attached in this way. One possibility is that

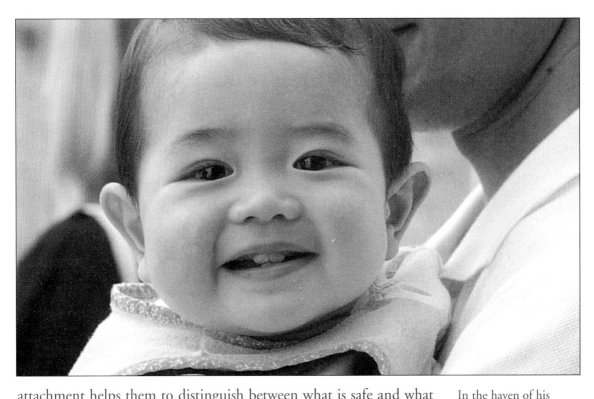

attachment helps them to distinguish between what is safe and what is dangerous; in other words, it is perhaps an evolutionary adaptation that protects babies from predators. But despite its adaptive nature, attachment can be a nuisance: the baby who starts to shriek uncontrollably at the sight of grandfather and grandmother – who may have come hundreds of miles for a first glimpse of their grandchild – can be a real embarrassment. Yet although attachment might look like an emotional regression, it is not. Only now – with her ability to represent people as individuals – can the baby begin to develop permanent, meaningful relationships. The diaries illustrate the interplay between attachment and fear of strangers:

In the haven of his father's arms, the nine-month-old will smile at passers-by, but at this age he may adamantly refuse to be held by a stranger.

> **Miranda (six months):** She smiles most of the time indiscriminately, though she's just becoming wary of strangers.

> **Amy (eight and a half months):** Amy is moderately clingy when we are at home or if we are out, if I am in sight. If I am out of sight and leave her with someone else (including my father in his surgery) she screams and cries non-stop. This stops the instant I reappear and she is all smiles when I pick her up.

> **Theo (nine months):** I have noticed that Theo behaves differently

with strangers depending on whether they have come to visit us or we are in an unfamiliar environment. Out of our flat, he will stare through people who make advances to him but at home he is much more flirtatious, especially if the person is friendly and relaxed but not too insistent.

(4 weeks later): Theo is now definitely unhappy about being held by strangers.

Eiki (ten months): He is now shy of strangers. He recognises his parents and those who are familiar to him. He does not want to be held by strangers. Two months ago he did not mind being held by strangers.

With father close by **(right)**, the child will confidently explore a new environment, but he will always keep within a radius of about a hundred feet as if joined to the father by an invisible thread …

The impact of attachment is not only negative – a sudden fear of strangers or of being abandoned. Attachment also has a positive effect. It gives the baby a safe base from which to explore the world. Paradoxically, the more the baby is attached, the more free she feels to explore the social and physical worlds. When she knows her mother or father is there to watch over her, the normally clinging baby is actually less fearful than a baby who has not yet shown attachment to her parents. The attached baby may crawl away from her parents for minutes at a time, but she always keeps them within a safe range and never strays beyond a radius of about a hundred feet. It is as if she were joined to her parent by an invisible thread. And the appearance of a stranger will stop her in her tracks and send her

… and, as if connected by a thread, he will constantly return to his father for reassurance before setting off again.

205

scuttling back to the haven of the familiar adult.

Attachment to mother – and anxiety at being separated from her – appear to be phenomena that occur in all cultures of the world. They are what are known as a developmental universals, like grasping, babbling, and other such behaviours. Studies have identified attachment and anxiety in children of roughly the same age in cultures as diverse as America, Botswana, Israel, and Guatemala. Long separations from mother during this period – as happen if a child has to be hospitalised – can have quite serious consequences. Not only do babies seem badly agitated during the period of separation, but they remain upset for long periods following reunion with mother. It is as if they continued to fear being separated again. Such negative repercussions have been observed in children of up to two or three years of age, although they tend generally to subside as children get older. With increased age, children usually grow more secure in the belief that their mother will not leave them permanently, even if they have to be temporarily separated. According to some theorists, this security acts as the basis for the child's ability to form attachments to all other people, and thus, to become an independent adult.

Babies' manner of reaction to separation has been the focus of much research, because it may provide a good index of attachment to mother. The 'Strange Situation' is a well-known procedure for arriving at such an index. The procedure is simple: the baby is taken into an unfamiliar room with mother. There are toys in the room, and the baby is allowed to play and to explore, with mother present all through. Once the baby is playing happily, a stranger comes into the room. He speaks to the mother and then approaches the child. Next, the mother leaves the room, so that the baby is left alone with the stranger. Finally, mother re-enters the room, and she is reunited with the baby.

How do one-year-old babies react to the 'Strange Situation'? Most babies can be classified as falling into one of three categories. Some two-thirds of babies can be categorised as 'securely attached'. These children play and explore so long as mother remains in the room, and they may even show some interest in the stranger. However, when the mother leaves, they become upset, and show real enthusiasm once she returns. A second group has been called 'insecurely attached – resistant'. These babies do not explore when mother is in the room, they panic and show great distress when she leaves, and they show mixed emotions upon her return. Babies in this group may do everything they can to be picked up, but then immediately fight to be put down again. Finally, the 'insecurely attached – avoidant' group are reserved and aloof at first, are not upset at mother's leaving, and pay no attention when she re-enters the room. Researchers have argued that these behaviour patterns remain stable over the first few years of life.

Some theorists have argued that children's behaviour in the 'Strange Situation' offers a good indicator of their relationship with their mother. And understanding how babies react in this situation is important, these theorists claim, because a child's relationship with her mother may be an important factor in determining her later emotional and social adjustment. On the other hand, other researchers disagree that early attachment to mother actually causes children to become either well- or maladjusted. These researchers point out, for example, that children's later adjustment may be caused simply by the child's own temperament, and not by the quality of the mother-child relationship. Some children may simply be inherently more sociable or irritable – and the 'Strange Situation' may actually be assessing what might be fixed traits in the child, rather than what has been built up by the attachment relationship.

It is interesting to note that the 'Strange Situation' has been used with both fathers and mothers. Babies did show some upset at father's departure from the room, and happiness at his return. However, overall babies showed considerably more distress when mother left the room, and they greeted her return with greater joy during this early period of development. Obviously such research has to be carried out afresh in today's modern family settings where fathers may be house-husbands and thus be more important to the baby.

Being attached allows the baby to develop many new behaviours, for example, laughing and clowning. Laughing may first occur in a situation that is potentially frightening, but which the baby knows to be safe because someone she trusts is present. When her father throws her up and down in the air, she may initially feel frightened. But she gradually relaxes as her father's smiling face reassures her that there's no danger. So what begins as a startled response to a scary situation progressively turns into a chuckle, as the diaries illustrate:

Joanne (seven months): Sometimes I wonder how much she really enjoys being tossed into the air by her grandpa. Sometimes it even scares me! She starts off by opening her mouth wide open as if she's going to vomit, but after a while she seems to enjoy it, and then she starts to make giggling noises.

Making others laugh is a means for the baby to sustain social interaction, and the positive reaction of others will encourage her to repeat her forays into the social world.

Only a few months later, laughter is no longer rooted in fear – it has become a pleasurable activity in itself. The baby's accidental discovery that her own mimicry can sometimes make others laugh may encourage her to do it over and over again, purely to amuse her audience. Although this clowning may not be a very sophisticated form of humour, it signals the beginning of purposeful control over her social environment and a dawning realisation that she can influence other people's mental states. This sort of behaviour may continue over quite a long period, as the diaries illustrate:

Taffy (nine and a half months): She makes kissing noises to make us laugh and repeats the action time after time. In fact, when I'm feeding her and perhaps should become a little stern she'll blow a kiss to make me laugh – I'm sure to ease the tension.

Sorsha (fifteen months): Sorsha has just started to do a funny little walk that makes us laugh. She pulls a face, shrugs her shoulders and brings her hands up then shuffles her feet. The more we laugh the more she does it!

Another humorous game which babies start to play at this age illustrates the beginnings of an understanding of their parents' eye gaze. A baby who crawls to a forbidden cupboard door may check whether or not her mother is watching before opening it and wreaking havoc with the pots and pans. Checking mother's eye gaze indicates that the baby knows that her mother needs to look where she is to know what she is up to. The diaries provide some nice examples of this new type of insight:

Thomas (seven and a half months): Attracted to all forbidden wires, plugs, etc. Looks at me first, then continues to head for them anyway!

Nadiyah (eight months): When Nadiyah doesn't want me to clean her nose, she blows bubbles (sort of spits!) at me to make me back off. This is exactly the reason for her doing it because when I do stop, she stops spitting, and when I start again so does she.

William (eleven months): He spends ages trying to open my bags and my Filofax. He will do it very quietly and knows it's naughty and jumps and looks guilty if I catch him.

Theo (eleven months): His new 'naughty' game is to climb up on the sofa in our bay window and then start attacking my plants on the window ledge. He knows he's not supposed to do it and looks at me with glee just before climbing up. He'll squeal as I come to remove him.

At this stage, the baby's interpretation of her parents' eye gaze is limited to checking where they are looking. It will be almost another full year before she understands *why* people look where they do – before she grasps the *intentions* conveyed by their eye gaze. As adults we constantly interpret the behaviour of others in terms of their intentions: she left the room because she wanted some water; he phoned me because he was lonely; he bought me a present because he was grateful. This way of thinking is different from simply noting other people's actions: the vase broke because she dropped it; the ice cream melted because she left it out of the freezer. And so the baby's learning to distinguish between actions and intentions is a crucial step in gaining an adult-like understanding of the social world.

Recent research with two- to three-year-olds looked at how children come to differentiate action from intention. The experimenter showed the children several simple line drawings of a face, called Charlie, whose eyes were looking in one of four directions: up to the right, down to the right, up to the left or down to the left. At each of the four corners of the page on which the face was drawn were replicas of different sweet packets: Mars Bar, Smarties, Polo Mints and Kit Kat. The children's task was very simple. Initially they had to answer the question: 'Where is Charlie looking?' No child had difficulty with that. They then had to answer a slightly different question: 'Which sweetie do you think Charlie wants?' The wording of this second question differs from the first in that it doesn't ask directly where Charlie is looking, but indirectly about his intention, that is, about what he wants. The children found this second question more difficult and often just guessed at what he wanted, thus showing that interpreting the meaning of facial expressions is not always immediate.

Understanding people's intentions from the direction of their eye gaze and other simple behaviour is a critical precursor to taking their perspective and understanding their feelings – abilities that are fundamental to survival in our complex social world. Such simple capacities give the child a growing sense of others.

A GROWING SENSE OF SELF

It was long thought that babies are born with no sense of themselves as separate entities, that they are unable to grasp the point where they end and others begin. None the less, very young babies can copy other people's facial gestures. We noted this form of imitation in our discussions in Chapter 1. If parents stick out their tongue or blink their eyes at a baby who is only a few hours old, the baby will often copy them. In this newborn behaviour, we see the seeds of social cognition – and the first dawnings of the distinction between self and others.

Over the course of the first year, the baby's reactions to her own reflection undergo a series of changes. Research has shown that prior to three months babies held up to a mirror show almost no interest in their own reflections or in the reflections of other people. At about four months, they will reach out and touch the mirror image if a toy or another person is reflected in it. But it is clear that they don't at this stage understand that they are seeing a reflection; they are

stretching out towards what they think are real objects or people. This is also clear from the fact that they don't look behind them when they see something approaching in the mirror. It is not until about ten to twelve months of age that babies will turn around if they see in the mirror that a toy is being slowly lowered behind their backs. They become fascinated by their own mirror images at this age, too. They seem to be happy to play with their own reflection for hours, as many of the entries in the parental diaries illustrate:

Very young infants may be fascinated with a mirror image, but it is unlikely that this baby knows it is himself in the mirror, or even that what he is seeing is not as 'solid' and 'real' as the world about him.

> **Amy (eight and a half months):** Amy has taken a leap forward in social skills. When she sees herself in a mirror she really is all smiles. She will even look at herself lovingly in the dark glass of the oven doors and she sometimes touches her image too.

> **Eiki (ten months):** He looks into the mirror and then he moves his head away from the mirror and then again he looks into the mirror, and looks at his own image and smiles. He repeats this again and again.

> **Marko (thirteen and a half months):** I watched the holiday video with Marko yesterday and he was mesmerised by himself. He doesn't usually watch TV but he didn't move from standing in

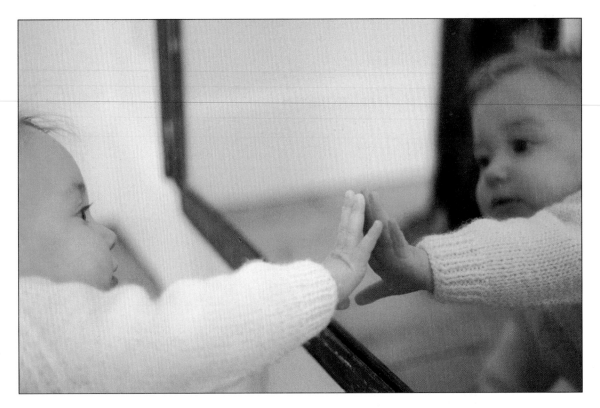

Once the baby is mobile he can experiment with mirror images. He will gradually gain a growing sense of self and slowly come to understand that it is himself he is seeing in the mirror.

front of it for half an hour. The whole video was mostly him, so it was very interesting to him.

It is not clear that the babies in the preceding examples actually recognise themselves; they may be simply responding to what looks like another interesting, smiling baby. Research findings seem to suggest that this might indeed be the case. At ten to twelve months, a baby may enjoy looking at herself in the mirror, but she still won't try to rub off a red spot that has been surreptitiously placed on her nose. It takes at least another six months before she becomes aware that the red spot on the nose of the mirror image must also be on her own nose; then she immediately tries to rub it off. Some examples from the developmental diaries suggest a new-found awareness of self from the way in which children behave with mirrors:

Sorsha (eighteen and a half months): Sorsha keeps kissing herself in the large mirror in the bedroom, then she waves and says 'Bye' when she leaves the room.

Collin (27 months): Loves his image in a mirror. Very coy with himself. Will often go in front of the mirror and watch himself talk, etc.

Gillian (32 months): Gillian's favourite game these days is sitting in front of the bathroom mirror. She seems to prefer it to her toys in the bath – sometimes she can sit for five minutes chatting away to herself, opening her mouth very wide as if she's studying the effect in the glass. Sometimes she'll pick up a brush and hold it up to the mirror, and then she'll look at the brush in her hand and then at the mirror. You can see she's really concentrating. I often hear her say 'Bye, Gilli' when she gets up to go out to the hall.

So the child's self-awareness has now developed to a point where she can readily recognise her own image in mirrors, videos and photographs. Fascinated by her own image, she has now also grasped the idea that she exists as an entity, with her particular attributes like

By the time the two-to three-year-old has a more developed sense of self, she delights in seeing distortions of her own image.

her own name. Naming herself is not a purely egotistical act; it's an expression of her new-found identity. With this new concept of self squarely in place, the toddler is ready to embark on the next leg of the journey toward becoming a social being.

INTERACTING WITH OTHERS

Despite the one-year-old's new sense of self and her ability to interact with those closest to her, her reaction to the people most like herself – other babies – illustrates how limited her social skills really are. She may seem interested in the infant brought into the room and placed on the floor opposite her – a newcomer who is just like herself. But she is very inept at interacting with this other child. At this age, babies rely almost entirely on their parents to initiate and sustain their social contact with others. Other children are treated more like inanimate objects than human beings, as the diaries show:

Despite the attractive object, the baby's attention is drawn to the world of people.

Amy (seven and a half months): Amy does not react to other babies other than to touch them as interesting objects. This usually means pulling their hair. She seems more interested in our cat, who

Despite the presence of a potentially interesting playmate, these babies still rely on adults to sustain their social interactions.

feels interestingly furry and can jump all around her in an interesting and unexpected way.

Thomas (eight months): Particularly fascinated by other children and wants to climb all over them and pull their hair and pat their heads and faces!

Izzy (eleven months): He reaches out and pulls on people's noses and hair.

Sorsha (fifteen months): In the shoe shop today, Sorsha came face to face with a boy about the same size as her. They were fascinated by each other but the little boy wanted to pull at her cheeks and

Even for the two-year-old, interaction with other children is still sporadic, and both may turn to the parent for support.

was very insistent. Sorsha didn't cry but tried to poke his eyes out and then gave him a big push. This carried on for about five minutes until the boy's mother came to get him. Sorsha then waved bye!

At about eighteen months, the toddler begins to spread her attachments around. She starts to socialise with other familiar people – relatives, neighbours, and family friends. Her offerings of food or toys to others may seem like acts of generosity, but they are actually attempts to get others to interact with her. She may hand a toy to another child and snatch it straight back, almost surprised that he has taken it! Or she may offer a half-eaten sandwich to a visiting adult! Such gestures are crude, but they are the only way that the baby knows of inviting people to join in her activities.

Toddlers of this age still don't know how to interact properly with their peers. They tend to engage in what is called 'parallel play'. They don't play together; they just stay close to one another and imitate each other's actions, as the diaries show:

Sorsha (fifteen and a half months): Sorsha met a friend in the park today, a little girl called Abbi aged twenty months, and she

Toddlers have a developed sense of social justice and turn-taking, but not the ability to sort things out by discussion. A good scream has a more immediate effect.

wanted to copy everything she was doing, stamping her feet, going on the roundabout, going on the swings, etc.

Yet the toddler's self-awareness opens up new possibilities: she can now pretend in order to try to get what she wants. She feigns being hungry to avoid going to bed or pretends to have hurt herself in order to get attention. This is not deception in the adult sense. The child is not trying to plant false ideas in the minds of others, but merely trying to affect their behaviour.

The diaries provide a couple of nice examples of this sort of behaviour:

Genevieve (21 months): She has been feigning crying when she wants something – usually to be picked up or helped with eating. She breaks into a grin when she gets what she wants.

(**One month later**): The 'phoney' cry is particularly in evidence this week, particularly since she caught a cold. She can turn it on and off almost instantly.

Rowan (23 months): She shows fake tears quite quickly that dry up immediately when she gets what she wanted.

Toddlers can also use their new understanding of other people's behaviour and feelings in positive ways – they can now really sympathise with people around them. They no longer simply react to happiness or sadness by smiling or looking downcast themselves. Instead, they may offer a caring gesture or a kind word. They can now understand how a brother could be upset, even though they cannot feel his pain directly. And they can foresee the possibility of making him feel better by using their own comforting behaviour. The child's concern for others is evident in the following examples:

Genevieve (21 months): Genny was looking at a book with her father, their heads literally together over it. Accidentally, both hit their heads against each other rather hard. When Genny finished crying over her own hurt head, she looked up at her dad and put her hand to his head.

Concern is evident, too, in this baby's reactions to her pregnant mother:

Natasha (30 months): Her thoughtfulness showed through today when she saw me struggling to get up. She put her hand out and offered to pull me up. She also stroked my back, saying 'Is your back sore, Mommy?'

BECOMING INDEPENDENT

Paradoxically, temper tantrums mark a positive stage in social development. They are a determined bid for independence. For some eighteen months, the baby has relied on her parents to do almost everything for her. Now that she has developed a strong sense of self, she wants to break free of parental care and control – to make her own decisions. Nightmarish though it may be for parents, this period – the 'terrible twos' – is crucial to the development of a mature concept of self. Here are three examples of children at this difficult stage of development:

Sorsha (sixteen months): Sorsha has been having tantrums today, first of all in Toys R Us as she wanted every toy in the shop. Even whilst I am trying to write this diary she is throwing things to me and trying to get my attention.

Danielle (seventeen months): The biggest tantrum this week was when she wanted a pushchair that a three-year-old was pushing. She pushed her over even though she was bigger than Danielle and grabbed the pram, and Danielle pushed it to the other end of the room.

Kaspar (25 months): Sometimes he has minor tantrums and half-way through forgets why he got upset!

When the social world falls apart the toddler turns to a parent for comfort.

221

'The terrible twos': the tantrums typical of this age group are actually a sign of a healthy, determined sense of self and a concerted bid for independence.

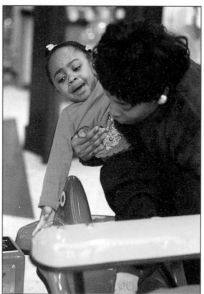

Although temper tantrums may seem to be no more than emotional outbursts, they actually represent children's growing awareness that they themselves can control what happens to them. They are becoming independent social beings.

THOUGHTS AND INTENTIONS IN OTHERS

An early indication that the child understands that other people have thoughts and beliefs of their own can be seen through the way she uses language. She starts to adapt her speech to the needs of others and to realise that they may not have shared the same experiences as she has. So when speaking to her mother she might use her sister's name, 'Jeannie', but when speaking to a stranger she might refer to Jeannie as 'my sister'. She will also start to realise that not everyone speaks as her parents do. She may therefore start to talk in one way to her mother and in another to the new baby. The diaries provide a telling example:

> **Alexandra (21 months):** On Monday we saw a friend who is seven months younger than Alexandra and I noticed she started to talk baby-talk with him and then speaking properly with us.

Research has documented this phenomenon. For example, pre-schoolers were recorded speaking both to another adult and to a child younger than themselves. The speech addressed to the younger child differed in crucial ways from that directed at the adult. When addressing the younger child, the pre-schoolers spoke more slowly, their pronunciation was clearer, their intonation more exaggerated, their words simpler and their sentences shorter. In fact, the speech pre-schoolers used for the younger child looked in many respects like 'motherese' – the special baby-talk that parents use and which we discussed in Chapter 4. Interestingly, all the pre-schoolers made these simplifications to their speech, even those who didn't have a younger sibling of their own. In other words, this capacity to adapt one's speech to others appears to be general to all children of this age. It is also important, because the ability to modify speech according to what other people know is fundamental to all successful social relationships.

Just as toddlers adapt their speech to people of different ages, so they adapt the words they use to people who speak different languages. The diaries provide a nice example:

> **Kaspar (27 months):** Kaspar started to use both English and German names for the same word and seems to know who to use them with: for example, he goes to the 'libree' (library) with my friend Deena and he goes to the 'tek' (*Bibliotek*) with me.

By the age of three, children clearly know rather a lot about other people. Yet there is good evidence that they still don't have a mature understanding of other people's mental states. They still seem to lack what developmental psychologists call a 'theory of mind'. Recall the difference we discussed earlier between knowing where someone is looking and knowing what his intentions are

From three years onwards, the child can attribute to others thoughts and feelings that are different to her own. It's an important intellectual and conceptual leap forward.

when looking in a particular direction. The ability to draw distinctions between intentions and actions, as well as to understand that others have beliefs, forms the roots of a theory of mind. But children also need to understand more complex intentions, like those based on false beliefs. A standard experimental task used to test children's understanding of false belief has several versions, one of which is as follows: a three-year-old is shown a tube that normally contains her favourite sweets. Asked what she thinks the tube contains, she says, 'Smarties!' The tube is then opened to reveal a surprise – it actually contains a pencil. The child is asked what the tube contains, and she of course then replies, 'A pencil'. The pencil is put back into the tube which is then closed. Next, the child is told that shortly her friend, who has not seen what is in the tube, will be coming into the room. The child is first asked, 'When you first saw the tube, what did you say it contained?', and she answers correctly: 'Smarties!' But when asked, 'When your friend comes in, what will he say the tube contains?', she answers incorrectly: 'A pencil!' In other words, three-year-olds often don't take into account the fact that others don't have the same knowledge as they do. They fail to see that other people's behaviour will be influenced by what they think is true, not necessary by what is true.

Three-year-olds' difficulty with false beliefs has been interpreted as an inability to understand that another person could hold a belief that the child knows is wrong. Although three-year-old children quite often fail tests like the Smarties task, only a year later they become capable of solving them. This result suggests that the period between three and four is important in the child's acquisition of a more mature 'theory of mind'.

But well before the child grasps the subtleties of her own and other

Copying the adult world initiates the baby into different social roles.

people's thoughts and feelings, she still finds the world of relationships and social rules fascinating. With her dolls, teddy-bears and nursery-school friends, the child relentlessly explores the world of people. Although she may at times seem like a mini-dictator, handing out much more punishment than praise, her disciplinary games are an important way of sorting out in her own mind the rules of her parents and of their society. Here are a couple of entries from the developmental diaries:

> **Collin (28 months):** Much of his interaction with other nursery children is telling himself and them what to do, i.e. 'don't run behind shed', 'no smack'.

> **Gillian (32 months):** Gillian's games are getting very vicious these days. I heard her the other day with her teddy bear, and wrote down what she was screaming: 'Right, Teddy, you're a bad boy, so I'll smack your face and you can't have no lunch. Bad, bad Teddy! You're not going out at playtime.' I don't know where she learns about smacking faces, certainly not at home. Maybe at the play centre.

MAKING FRIENDS

Between two and three, the child's new-found social understanding opens the door to making friends with the people in the world who are most like herself: other children. She finally knows how to initiate a conversation with her peers and how to play games in a reciprocal way. The relationships she forms at this point may be based more on shared interests in the here-and-now than on any lasting emotional ties. A 'friendship' made within five minutes in a supermarket is unlikely to be the start of a life-long relationship! The diaries illustrate the tenuous nature of these early friendships:

> **Stacey (24 months):** She seems to chop and change her so-called 'friends' on a daily basis!

> **Gillian (33 months):** Gillian is quite muddled about what real friendships are. We were talking about a little girl at the nursery, Mary, and she commented: 'No, she's not my friend, she's my best friend'! But two days later she said that Mary was horrid and not her friend at all.

> **Janet (37 months):** J. plays for hours with the little boy next door and then insists she doesn't like him, only girls are her friends.

Nonetheless, the child has begun to grasp one of the most important aspects of being human: how to relate to and cooperate with other people. The diaries provide an example of this cooperative behaviour which will increasingly characterise children's development over the coming years:

> **Collin (28 months):** He has become more understanding of the rules about playing with other children. If he is caught taking a toy away from a child and it is explained why he must return it, he will do so and say 'sorry'. He can now understand what it feels like to have some empathy.

> **(One month later):** We're able to reason with Collin much easier now. If we ask him to wait for something, he will do so and remind us of our promise every so often.

In less than 36 months, the baby has become a walking, talking, tool-using, thinking, social being. But the journey is far from over.

As children get older their games become more elaborate and social: each child has a separate role, which fits into the scenario of the shared game.

A friendship made in five minutes may not last a lifetime but for the time being it is a deep social bond, beyond the world of adults (**opposite**). In the short space of thirty-six months, these two have grown from helpless, uncoordinated babies into walking, talking, tool-using people, capable of social interaction and abstract thought.

The child can walk, but she's no Martina Navratilova; the child can use tools, but she's no Picasso; the child has language, but she's no Shakespeare; the child can experiment, but she's no Einstein; and the child can feel sympathy, but she's no Florence Nightingale! Few children will end up reaching these extraordinary heights. But most will use their first three years of life as a springboard from which to learn to run a race and ride a bicycle, to mend the garden fence and paint the house, to tell long stories and write to a penfriend, to fathom how the hi-fi works and programme a computer, to bandage a wound and take someone's temperature. And they will soon take those early years for granted and forget just how hard they once worked when they were still at play!

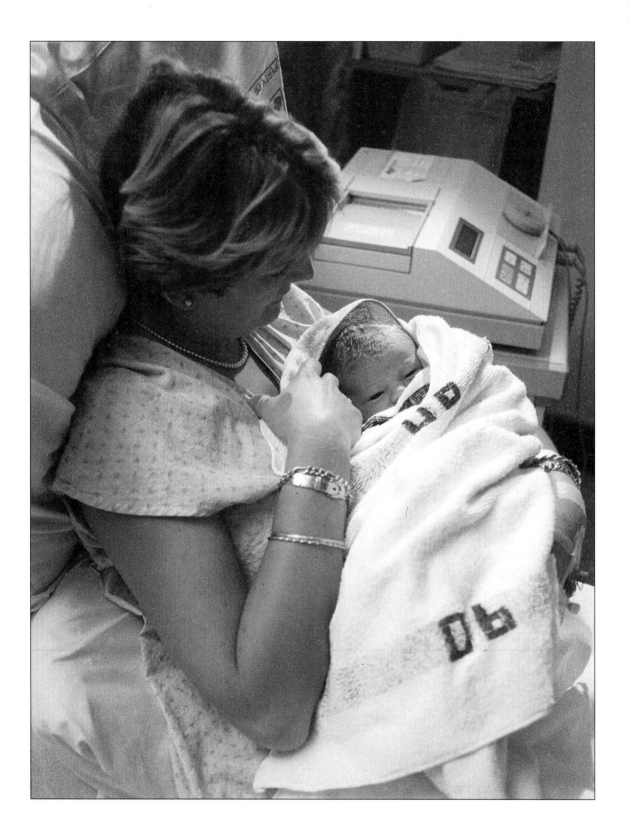

EXPERIMENTAL TECHNIQUES USED WITH YOUNG INFANTS

Throughout the book, mention was made of experiments which have revealed unsuspected capacities in the newborn and young infant. Three particularly useful techniques have been devised. Two fall under the habituation/dishabituation paradigm; the third uses preferential looking (or preferential listening).

Take the infant's sensitivity to shape as an example. In the habituation/dishabituation paradigm, infants are presented repeatedly with pictures of squares on a screen. The squares vary in size and colour each time. After a while the newborn shows decreasing interest in squares, despite constant variations in size and colour. She looks less and less and shows signs of boredom. Then a circle is presented. If the infant continues to show lack of interest on presentation of the circle, then it can be concluded that the baby sees the circle as equivalent to the squares, i.e. that shape discrimination is a later achievement. By contrast, if the newborn shows sudden renewed interest on presentation of a circle and looks at it longer, then one can conclude that shape discrimination is present at birth and does not have to be learned. In fact, it is present at birth. The same experimental logic is used to test discriminations of other types of stimuli. By clever manipulation of features such as shape, colour, size, number, and so forth, the researcher can discover the nature of the difference to which the infant is sensitive.

Another example comes from the infant's sensitivity to size constancy. Take any object in your hand at arms length, and then move it slowly towards your face. You will see that the object *seems* to get larger and larger, and indeed the size of the object on your retina *is*

Far left: it is during the first couple of hours after birth that initial experiments and tests with newborns are carried out.

231

larger. But you know of course that the object remains the same size throughout. You have what is called 'size constancy'. The question is whether newborn babies also have size constancy and how to devise an experiment to test this. The habituation technique was used again. Like the experiment with squares and circles described above, here too babies were shown a series of one display until they got bored, and then a new display was shown. First two identical balls – of the same diameter and at the same distance from the baby – were shown until the baby got bored. Then one of two events was shown. One group of babies was shown two balls at the same distance as before, except that one of the balls was considerably larger than the other – a new event. Another group of babies was shown the original two balls, except that this time one of the two balls was much closer to the baby and so it *appeared* to be considerably larger although it was actually the same size – another new event. Would the babies consider both new events as different from the original event? In fact, they did not. The group who in fact saw different-sized balls renewed its interest and suddenly started to look longer. By contrast, the group for whom the balls were actually the same size and one just appeared larger did not renew their interest. They clearly considered the new event to be the same as the original one. In other words, the results from this group of babies showed that size constancy is part of the equipment with which the baby is born.

Infants have also been shown to be sensitive to number. Infants are presented repeatedly with sets of two objects (say, a picture of two bears, followed by a picture of two dogs, followed by a picture of two birds, etc.) until they show lack of interest (i.e. start to attend to the display for shorter times). Then a different stimulus is presented (a picture of three cats). So infants are habituated to two-object displays until they get bored, and then shown a three-object display. Recall that each stimulus display is different, so the infant could simply be fascinated with a series of pictures of different animals, and totally disregard how many are being shown. But this is not what happens. Rather rapidly infants start to show boredom when yet another picture of two animals (albeit different ones) is shown. However, when a picture of three animals is displayed, infants' attention is suddenly renewed. From this we can assume that they noticed the difference in number. To adults, the difference between two and three may seem a very simple one, but when we are talking of a three month old's sensitivity to numerical differences, the results are truly striking.

Far right: babies are fascinated by moving objects and will swipe at them whenever possible.

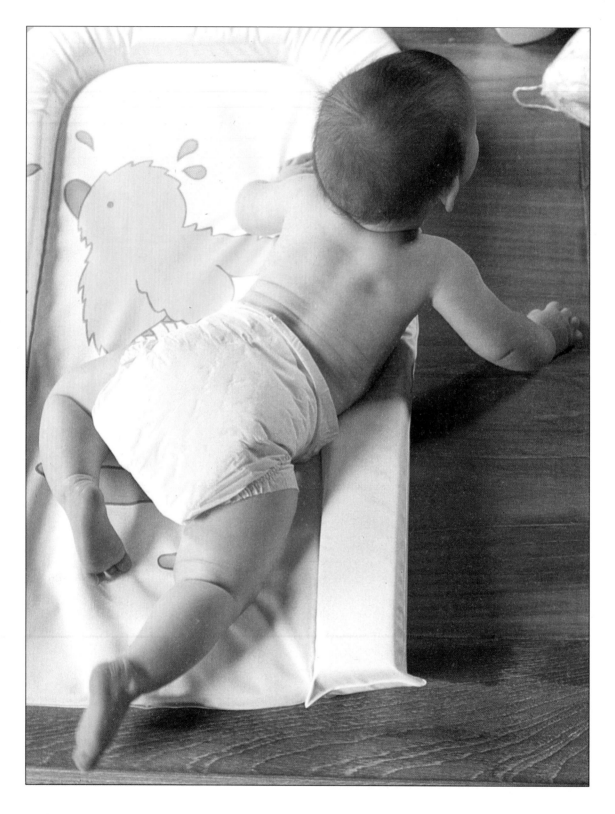

These techniques can also be used with older babies. For example, research has probed young infants' sensitivity to the laws of gravity. Infants are first shown a ball released at the top of a screen and then watch it descend slowly until it reaches a platform. They see this over and over again until they start to get bored. Then they are shown one of two events. One group of babies sees the ball stop in mid-air with a hand holding it. The other group of babies sees a similar event but this time the ball stops in mid-air without anything holding it. Do both groups of babies interpret the event in the same way? In fact not. The babies who see the ball stop mid-air without any support look longer than the other group. They have detected something unusual in the physical world. But this is not present at birth. It is the result of learning and is only to be seen in the second half of the first year. Likewise with acceleration and deceleration. Babies were first shown normal events – a ball going up a hill and its speed gradually decreasing, or a ball going down a hill and its speed gradually increasing. They watched such events until they showed boredom. Babies who saw the upward event were then either shown the downward event – another different but normal event – or an 'impossible' event – the ball's speed *increased* as it went up the hill. Once again the experimental technique allowed researchers to make interesting conclusions. Babies who saw different but normal events quickly got bored again. By contrast, babies who saw the 'impossible' event suddenly renewed their interest.

Two kinds of response are used to measure 'boredom' or 'interest': varying amplitude of sucking or varying length of looking. We've just looked briefly at some examples of the varying length of looking measure. Babies look longer when they think they are seeing something new, but they look for shorter and shorter spells when they are bored with what they judge to be the same thing. In the case of varying amplitutde of sucking, the infant is given a non-nutritive dummy or pacifier to suck, which is attached to an apparatus that measures variations in sucking amplitude. This technique has been used to see whether infants are sensitive to changes in sounds, e.g., whether infants can hear the difference between, say, /ra/ and /la/. As infants habituate to repeated presentations of /ra/ (i.e., get bored with hearing that sound), their sucking amplitude decreases. When the stimulus changes to /la/, if they notice the difference, their sucking amplitude will suddenly increase. By contrast, if the infant were to hear /ra/ and /la/ as the same sound (as Japanese adults do), then sucking amplitude would plateau or continue to decrease. We

When the baby first starts to roll, she can perceive depth but is in no fear of it (**far left**) – this baby could easily roll off the table if not watched carefully. However, fear of depth develops about two weeks after the baby learns to crawl – just when she needs it most.

discussed this example in Chapter 1.

A third infancy paradigm involves preferential looking. Here, habituation/dishabituation curves are not measured. Instead, infants are presented with two stimulus displays simultaneously, and measurement is taken of which display they prefer to look at. Such a technique has been used to measure infants' capacity to match the number of auditory stimuli (e.g., three drum beats) to the number of toys in either of two screens, one showing two toys, the other three. Six- to eight-month-olds look intently at two-object displays when they hear two drum beats, and at three-object displays when they hear three drum beats. The same technique can be used to see how much of language babies understand before they themselves can produce more than single words. Babies are played a sentence from a loudspeaker and see two screens showing animated films, one screen showing an action matching the sentence and the other showing the same characters doing something different. Babies could simply flip their attention to and fro between the screens. But if instead they look much longer at the screen matching the sentence they heard from the loudspeaker, then we can conclude that they understand something about its meaning. We discussed such examples in Chapter 4.

All of these techniques can be used to reveal the extraordinary capacities of young infants.

Far right: it takes great coordination, muscular strength and balance for the baby to be able to grasp a toy while supporting himself in a sitting position.

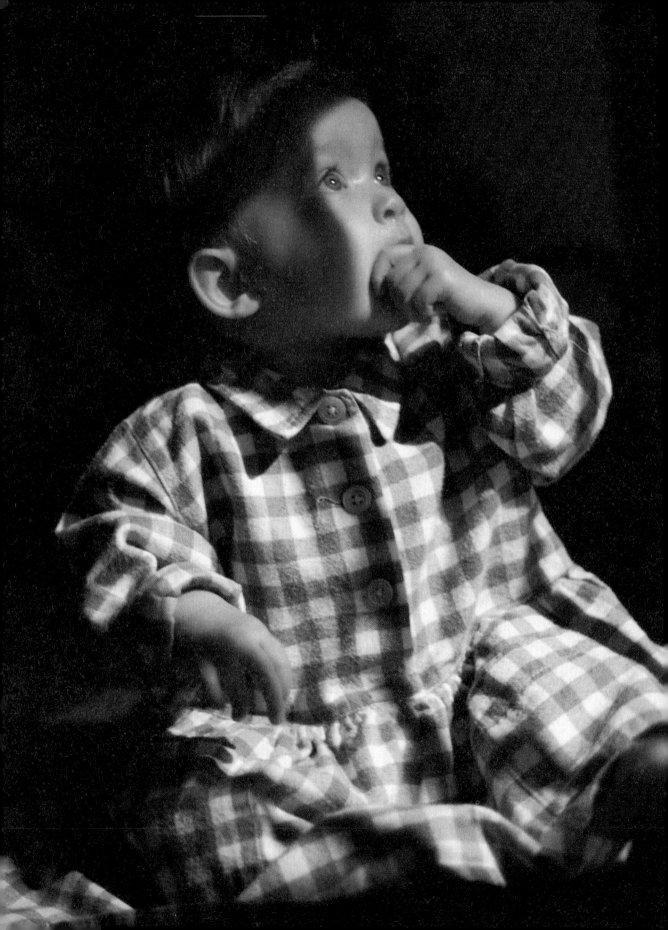

DEVELOPMENTAL DIARY QUESTIONNAIRE

This questionnaire was used to follow the progress of the babies filmed for the television series. When completed every week, the questionnaire provides a fascinating picture of the astonishing changes and development undergone by the young baby.

General behaviour patterns
What are your baby's sleeping and feeding patterns at the moment? What times of the day is s/he most alert? When does s/he have naps/go to bed at night/wake up in the morning?

Mobility: your child's developing ability to get from A to B
How does your baby move? How does s/he kick? Can s/he sit up

Getting to know each other – the baby already appears to be programmed with a 'template' of the human face.

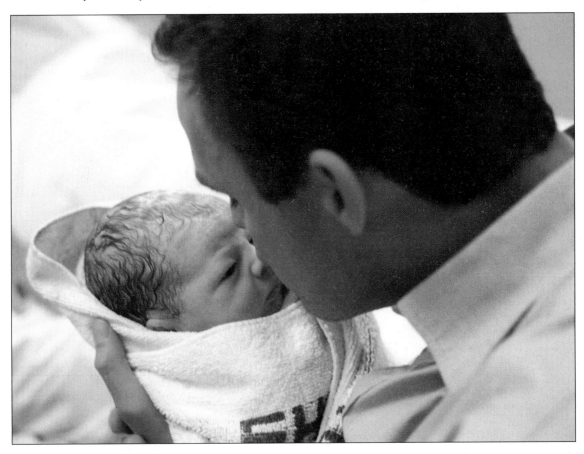

Though unable to speak, the nine-to-ten-month-old baby is capable of understanding much of what is going on about him.

with or without cushions? Does s/he roll around a lot? What style of crawling has s/he developed (bum-shuffle, commando crawl)? Does s/he pull on people or furniture to stand up? Do you arrange furniture so that s/he can 'cruise' around rooms holding on? How does s/he go down stairs? How is s/he walking now? Running/jumping/dancing/clambering up climbing frames?

Dexterity: your child's developing ability to manipulate tools

How does your baby use its eyes at the moment? Does s/he study own hands? How does s/he grasp objects? Is s/he transferring objects from one hand to the other? Banging things together? How does s/he feed her/himself? How exactly does s/he pick up very small things like raisins? What other things around the house does s/he open (including doors)? How does s/he hold pencils or crayons? How easily does s/he put on/do up/take off clothes?

Communication: your child's developing ability to communicate

What kind of cries does your baby make? Does s/he blow bubbles? Does s/he coo to her/himself? Does s/he use his/her eyes to get your attention? What kind of singsong single-vowel sounds ('da' or 'goo' for example)? Is s/he making tuneful babbling sounds ('da da da ga ga ga' etc.)? When is the most vocal time of day? Does s/he respond to 'yes' and 'no' commands? What is your child's first word (own 'jargon')? Does s/he point at things for you to name? Does s/he speak long sentences in own language? What understandable words is s/he using ('car', 'cat', 'duck' etc.)? Does s/he combine pointing plus a word to make up a bigger sentence? How many words does s/he use? What grammatical mistakes is s/he making? What other examples of your child's verbal or non-verbal communication have you noticed?

Problem solving: your child's developing ability to think

Does your baby react to routines? Which ones? Can s/he shake a rattle to make it sound? Does s/he listen for your footsteps? How does your baby explore new objects? Can s/he find an object if you hide it under a cloth? What happens if you put a toy in a box and close the lid – can s/he get the toy out again or copy you putting it in? Can s/he match shapes well enough to complete a very simple jigsaw? Does s/he like building blocks just so that s/he can knock them down again – i.e. does s/he understand that s/he can make things happen? Does s/he copy domestic tasks like hoovering,

This toddler is hearing the sound of her own voice for the first time.

sweeping? Is your child able to name things in the kitchen or bathroom while s/he is somewhere else? What kind of messy things does s/he enjoy? Does s/he 'pretend' play with you, or alone? What other examples of your child's thoughtfulness have you observed?

Social: your child's developing social skills

When does your baby smile? How does s/he let you know that s/he is enjoying certain routines? What situations have made your child anxious? When does s/he laugh? When is s/he affected by your moods? Does s/he react to mirror images or photos/videos of her/himself? What type of 'peek-a-boo' games does s/he enjoy? Does s/he wave goodbye to people yet? Is s/he clingy around strangers? How has your child been naughty? What instigated the biggest tantrum? What is his/her reaction to other children of the same age? How long will s/he play alone when other people are nearby? Does s/he share toys with other children? What kind of games does s/he play with other kids – what do they do and say?

Other

Just jot down anything else you think is necessary! What did s/he do this week to surprise you? How did s/he make people laugh? What out-of-the-home places have inspired him or her?

At nine to ten months, babies can become very 'clingy' and attached to their parents.

FURTHER READINGS

Anderson, M. (1992). *Intelligence and Development: A cognitive theory.* Oxford: Blackwell.

Bee, H. (1992) *The Developing Child* (6th Ed.) New York: Harper Collins.

Bremner, G.(1988) *Infancy.* Oxford: Blackwell.

Boden, M. (1979) *Piaget.* London: Fontana.

Clarke-Stewart, A. (1993). *Daycare.* Cambridge MA: Harvard University Press, The Developing Child Series.

Cole, M. and Cole, S.R. (1989) *The Development of Children.* New York: Freeman

Crystal, D. (1986) *Listen to Your Child: A Parent's Guide to Children's Language.* Harmondsworth: Penguin.

Dunn, J. (1988) *The Beginnings of Social Understanding.* Oxford: Blackwell.

Field, T. (1990) *Infancy.* Cambridge MA: Harvard University Press, The Developing Child Series.

Garvey, C. (1977). *Play.* Cambridge MA: Harvard University Press, The Developing Child Series.

Harris, P. (1989) *Children and Emotion: The Development of Psychological Understanding.* Oxford: Blackwell.

Johnson, M.H. and Morton, J. (1991) *Biology and Cognitive Development: The Case of Face Recognition.* Oxford: Blackwell.

Karmiloff-Smith, A. (1992) *Beyond Modularity: A Developmental Perspective on Cognitive Science.* Cambridge, Mass: MIT Press/ Bradford Books.

Lee, V. and DasGupta, P. (1994) *Children's Cognitive and Language Development.* Oxford: Blackwell.

Mehler, J. and Dupoux, E. (1994) *What Infants Know.* Oxford: Blackwell.

Oakes, J. (1994) *Foundations of Development.* Oxford: Blackwell.

Parke, R. (1981). *Fathers.* Cambridge MA: Harvard University Press, The Developing Child Series.

Rutkowska, J. *The Computational Infant.* Hemel Hemstead: Harvester Wheatsheaf.

Schaffer, R. (1985). *Mothering.* Cambridge MA: Harvard University Press, The Developing Child Series.

Slater, A. and Bremner, J.G. (Eds.), (1993). *The Psychology of Infancy.* Hillsdale, NJ: Erlbaum.

Slater, A. and Bremner, B (Eds.) *(1989) Infant Development.* Hillsdale, NJ: Erlbaum.

Stern, D. (1977) *The First Relationship: Infant and Mother.* Cambridge MA: Harvard University Press, The Developing Child Series.

de Villiers, P. and de Villiers, J. (1979). *Early Language.* Cambridge MA: Harvard University Press, The Developing Child Series.

ACKNOWLEDGEMENTS

The writings and research of the following people inspired either directly or indirectly both the television series of *Baby It's You* and this book, and they are most gratefully acknowledged:

K. Adolf, M. Ainsworth, M. Anderson, J. Astington, J. Atkinson, T. Au, R. Baillargeon, M. Baldwin, M. Banks, S. Baron-Cohen, J. Bartrip, E. Bates, P. Bauer, A. Bell, U. Bellugi, J. Belsky, B. Bertenthal, E. Bialystock, E. Blehar, L. Bloom, P. Bloom, O. Braddick, M. Braine, M. Brami-Mouling, G. Bremner, J. Brooks-Gunn, A. Brown, J. Bruner, P. Bryant, I. Bushnell, G. Butterworth, W. Callender, R. Campbell, J. Campos, S. Carey, C. Cazden, E. Clark, R. Clifton, L. Cohen, M. Cole, S. Cole, R. Cowan, S. Crain, D. Crystal, P. Dale, M. DasGupta, A. Diamond, J. Dockrell, M. Donaldson, J. Dunn, S. Dziurawiec, P. Eimas, H. Feldman, E. Ferreiro, K. Fischer, U. Frith, K. Fuson, R. Gallistel, R. Gelman, L-A. Gerken, E. Gibson, H. Gleitman, L. Gleitman, S. Goldin-Meadow, R. Golinkoff, J-C. Gomez, M. Goodale, J. Goodnow, A. Gopnik, C. Granrud, P. Greenfield, W. Greenough, M. Haith, G. Hall, P. Harris, M. Heimann, S.Henderson, P. Hepper K. Hirsh-Pasek, C. von Hofsten, F. Horowitz, B. Inhelder, J. Janowsky, J. Johnson, M. Johnson, P. Jusczyk, J. Kagan, A. Karmiloff-Smith, S. Keeble, R. Kermoian, E. Klima, M. Kotelchuk, P. Kuhl, F. Lacerda, B. Landau, K. Lee, A. Leslie, C. Lewis, M. Lewis, J. Macnamara, M. Malakoff, J. Mandler, V. Marchman, E. E. Markman, D. Maurer, J. McShane, M. McTear, J. Mehler, A. Meltzoff, D. Messer, J. Morton, R. Most, N. Myers, K. Nelson, H. Neville, E. Newport, L. Oakes, H. Papousek, L. Petitto, J. Perner, J. Piaget, S. Pinker, H. Poizner, M. Posner, C. Pratt, D. Premack, D. Olson, V. Reddy, R. Remez, B. Rogoff, E. Rolls, C. Rovee-Collier, J. Rutskowska, R. Schaffer, A. Schlottman, S. de Schonen, T. Schultz, M. Shatz, E. Shipley, A. Slater, C. Smith, C. Snow, N. Soja, C. Sophian, E. Spelke, D. Spring, P. Starkey, I. St James-Roberts, M. Strauss, J. Sullivan, H. Hager-Flusberg, M. Taylor, D. Thal, A. Teberosky, R. Thatcher, E. Thelen, L. Tolchinsky-Landsman, C. Trevarthen, G. Turkewitz, I. Uzgiris, V. Valian, A. Vinter, S. Wall, M. Waters, J. Watson, S. Waxman, R. Weir, P. Willats, H. Wimmer, P. Wolff, K. Wynn.

INDEX